SIMPLY THE BEST
TRI-GRILL/GRIDDLE RECIPES
MARIAN GETZ

INTRODUCTION BY WOLFGANG PUCK

ACKNOWLEDGMENTS

A most sincere thank you to our wonderful viewers and customers for without you there would be no need for a cookbook. I try very hard to give you an array of recipes suited for the particular kitchen tool the cookbook is written for. Wolfgang and I create recipes faster than we can write them down. That is what chefs do and is also the reason to tune in to the live shows and even record them so you can learn new dishes that may not be in our cookbooks yet.

Thank you most of all to Wolfgang. You are the most passionate chef I know and it has been a privilege to work for you since 1998. You are a great leader and friend. Your restaurants are full of cooks and staff that have been with you for 20 or more years which is a true testament to how you lead us. Thanks for allowing me to write these cookbooks and for letting me share the stage at HSN with you.

To Greg, my sweet husband since 1983. Working together is a dream and I love you. You have taught me what a treasure it is to have a home filled with people to laugh with.

To my sons, Jordan and Ben, we have a beautiful life, don't we? It just keeps on getting better since we added Lindsay, J. J., precious Easton and our second grand baby Sadie Lynn.

To all the great people at WP Productions, Syd, Arnie, Mike, Phoebe, Michael, Nicolle, Tracy, Genevieve, Gina, Nancy, Sylvain and the rest of the team, you are all amazing to work with. Watching all the wonderful items we sell develop from idea to final product on live television is an awe-inspiring process to see and I love that I get to be a part of it.

To Daniel Koren, our patient editor and photographer, thank you for your dedication. You make the photo shoot days fun and you are such an easygoing person to work with in the cramped, hot studio we have to share. We have learned so much together and have far more to learn.

To Greg, Cat, Estela, Angi, Laurie, Keith, Margarita and Maria who are the most dedicated, loving staff anyone could wish for. You are the true heroes behind the scenes. You are a well-oiled machine of very hard working people who pull off the live shows at HSN. It is a magical production to watch, from the first box unpacked, to the thousands of eggs cracked and beaten to running to get that "thing" Wolf asks for at the last minute, to the very last dish washed and put away it is quite a sight to behold. I love you all and I deeply love what we do.

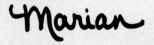

In today's modern kitchen, there are numerous types of appliances at your disposal. This also holds true in my restaurants. The real estate in your home kitchen is just as valuable to that of a restaurant kitchen. Neither needs an appliance that can only do one thing. We need and want appliances that are capable of doing several different tasks.

The Tri-Grill/Griddle is the perfect multi-tasker. It can make anything from breakfast to lunch to dinner, even snacks. The nonstick cooking surfaces, adjustable positions, independent temperature controls and different cooking plates allow for preparing sandwiches, meats, vegetables and even desserts.

Marian's "Simply The Best Tri-Grill/Griddle Recipes" cookbook is the perfect match for my Tri-Grill/Griddle. She has done an amazing job at writing recipes that will even make a novice cook fell like a pro. Over the years, Marian has proven to me to be a very reliable resource. I admire her experience in the kitchen, both in the restaurant and at home. While she likes making challenging dishes, she is also comfortable preparing everyday meals that her family loves to eat. The Tri-Grill/Griddle is perfect for making both, which lead her to writing this cookbook.

As I learned long ago, alongside my mother and grandmother, you should always put lots of love into everything you cook. This is certainly evident in this cookbook.

Wolfgang Puck

INTRODUCTION BY WOLFGANG PUCK

RECIPES

TABLE OF CONTENTS

TRI-GRILL/GRIDDLE TIPS

PREHEATING

Preheating your Tri-Grill is very important to the desired outcome of the food you are preparing. Preheating for 5 minutes will help you achieve the most even cooking. A well preheated grill is especially important when searing foods. A steak or chicken breast will start steaming instead of cooking if the Tri-Grill has not been preheated to its maximum temperature.

Because the preheat time of your Tri-Grill is quite short, it is recommended to plan ahead. If you know a recipe has many steps or lots of chopping, don't plug in the Tri-Grill until shortly before you plan to use it. This will also help you save energy.

STICKING

Use a nonstick cooking spray as needed to control sticking. These sprays contain lecithin, which is made from soybeans and is one of the best nonstick agents available. You will notice that as you continue to use your Tri-Grill, you will be able to use less nonstick spray. This is because the plates are getting seasoned and become more naturally nonstick with repeated use.

MULTI-TASKING

When you are grilling meats on your Tri-Grill, add vegetables or even fruit so that the entire meal comes off of this wonderful appliance. The interchangeable plates and different positions will allow you to be flexible and cook multiple items at the same time. Use the CONTACT position to cook faster by allowing both plates to contact the food. Use the FIXED position when you do not want the upper plate to come in contact with your food like when melting cheese, heating a sauce on top of your cooked food or when cooking delicate items that you do not want compressed. Utilizing your Tri-Grill to its full potential will allow you to make your meals faster and have less cleanup.

CLEANING

For easier cleanup, I like to place a triple layer of wet paper towels on my Tri-Grill right after unplugging it. Close the lid and let the moisture from the wet paper towels steam off the stuck-on food. Afterwards, use the paper towels to quickly wipe over cooking plates and clean up will be done in no time.

SEASONING

Always remember to season your foods appropriately before cooking. Well-seasoned meat or vegetables are often the only difference between badly cooked foods at home and delicious foods cooked at your favorite restaurant. Seasoning can be as simple as adding some oil, salt and pepper or a bit of pesto for an easy burst of flavor. Season every bite by sprinkling the seasonings evenly over the surface of the food. It's all about the right balance.

PREP ONCE - USE TWICE

When slicing peppers or onions, slice some extra and keep them refrigerated in sealed containers. This will help you save time when preparing the next meal. If you are really busy, you can purchase the pre-sliced and chopped vegetables at your grocery store.

COOK ONCE - EAT TWICE

Whenever I grill some chicken, beef or vegetables on my Tri-Grill, I like to grill some extra so that the leftovers are ready to be sliced and tossed into a yummy salad, wrap or pasta. Cooking once and eating twice is a great time and energy saver that is one of the best ways to buy back a bit of time from an already busy schedule.

SAVE CALORIES

If you are trying to save some calories when making sandwiches, use a bit of nonstick cooking spray on the outside of the sandwiches instead of oil or butter. To add some flavor, make a small cup of flavorful broth using bouillon and a minced garlic clove. Use this broth for dipping the same way you would a French Dip sandwich. It is delicious.

RAW MEAT

When cooking raw meat, be mindful of what you do with your tongs. If you use the same pair of tongs to place the raw chicken on the Tri-Grill then later use them to transfer the cooked chicken to a platter, there is a chance that those tongs may still have live bacteria on them. Either wash them before removing cooked food or use a second pair.

PANTRY TIPS

Being prepared to cook the recipes in this book, or any recipe for that matter, is one of the keys to success in the kitchen. Your pantry must be stocked with the basics. We all know how frustrating it can be when you go to the cupboard and what you need is not there. This list includes some of the ingredients you will find in this book and some that we feel are important to always have on hand.

PERISHABLES:

Onions
Garlic
Tomatoes
Carrots
Celery
Ginger
Bell Peppers
White Potatoes
Sweet Potatoes
Squashes
Citrus
Apples
Bananas
Lettuce
Spinach
Fresh Herbs
Green Onions
Milk
Cream Cheese
Parmesan Cheese
Yogurt
Other Cheeses You Like

SPICES:

Kosher Salt
Pepper
Bay Leaves
Sage
Oregano
Thyme
Chili Flakes
Cumin Seeds
Curry Powder
Onion Powder
Garlic Powder
Dry Mustard
Ground Cinnamon
Nutmeg
Cloves
Chili Powder

DRY GOODS:

Sugars
Sugar Substitute
Vanilla
Extracts/Flavorings
Agave Syrup
Canned Tomatoes
Canned Beans
Canned Vegetables
Dried Chilies
Pasta
Lentils
Stocks
Powdered Bouillon
Olives
Ketchup
Mustard
Pickles
Oils
Vinegar
Honey

It is not necessary to have all the items listed at all times. However, if you are feeling creative, adventurous or just following a recipe, it's great to have a good selection in the kitchen.

CHEESE STEAK
SANDWICH

Makes 2 servings

Ingredients:

6 ounces rib eye steak, thinly sliced
1/2 green bell pepper, julienned
1/2 yellow onion, julienned
Kosher salt and fresh pepper to taste
2 hoagie rolls, split
4 cheese slices of your choice

Method:

1. Fit the Tri-Grill with the upper and lower RIBBED GRILLING PLATES then set to CONTACT position.
2. To preheat, set the upper and lower temperature to 450°F.
3. Place half of the steak, peppers and onions on the Tri-Grill.
4. Season with salt and pepper then close lid.
5. Cook for 2-3 minutes or until desired doneness (meat will not be very brown).
6. Transfer to a bottom hoagie roll half then top with 2 cheese slices.
7. Cover with top hoagie roll half then place back on the Tri-Grill; close lid.
8. Cook for 2 minutes to warm through and toast the hoagie roll.
9. Remove then repeat with remaining ingredients.

TIP

This sandwich is also great made with chicken. To thinly slice the chicken, freeze it for 30 minutes before slicing.

INDIVIDUAL MEATLOAF

Makes 4 servings

For The Meatloaf:

1 pound lean ground beef
1 small yellow onion, minced
1 large egg, beaten
1 bread slice, torn into small bits
2 tablespoons whole milk
1 tablespoon yellow mustard
1/4 cup bottled BBQ sauce
1 teaspoon dried sage
1 teaspoon kosher salt
1/4 teaspoon freshly ground black pepper

For Serving:

Soft buns
Bottled BBQ sauce
Dill pickle slices
Slivered red onions

Method:

1. *Fit the Tri-Grill with the upper and lower RIBBED GRILLING PLATES then set to CONTACT position.*
2. *To preheat, set the upper and lower temperature to 450°F.*
3. *In a bowl, combine all meatloaf ingredients; mix well.*
4. *Divide mixture into 4 equal patties.*
5. *Place 2 patties on the Tri-Grill; close lid.*
6. *Cook for 4 minutes or until desired doneness.*
7. *Remove then repeat with remaining patties.*
8. *Serve with soft buns, desired toppings and condiments.*

TIP

One of my favorite side dishes to this speedy little meatloaf is taking leftover baked potatoes, slicing them into 1-inch thick planks, brushing them with olive oil then seasoning them with salt and pepper before putting them on the Tri-Grill for 1-2 minutes. Simply delicious.

RECIPES

GRILLED FISH

Makes 4 servings

Ingredients:

4 fillets white fish, such as cod
2 tablespoons fresh ginger, minced
4 garlic cloves, minced
2 tablespoons soy sauce
1 tablespoon honey
2 teaspoons dark sesame oil
1 bunch scallions, thinly sliced
1/2 bunch cilantro, chopped
Pinch of chili flakes (optional)
Cooked rice for serving
Jalapeño peppers, diced

Method:

1. *Fit the Tri-Grill with the upper and lower RIBBED GRILLING PLATES then set to CONTACT position.*
2. *To preheat, set the upper and lower temperature to 350°F.*
3. *Pat fish thoroughly dry using paper towels.*
4. *In a small bowl, combine the ginger, garlic, soy sauce, honey, oil, scallions, cilantro and chili flakes if desired; stir.*
5. *Brush or spoon 1/2 of the ginger mixture over all sides of the fish; reserve remaining ginger mixture for serving.*
6. *Apply nonstick cooking spray to the Tri-Grill.*
7. *Place 2 fish fillets on the Tri-Grill; close lid.*
8. *Cook for 3-4 minutes or until well browned.*
9. *Remove when fish flakes easily but is still moist inside.*
10. *Repeat with remaining fish fillets.*
11. *Serve hot over rice with reserved ginger sauce and topped with jalapeño peppers.*

TIP

When making the ginger mixture, make some extra for later use. This delicious mixture freezes beautifully and is a great flavor boost to many meals without much hassle.

EGGPLANT STACK

Makes 2 servings

Ingredients:

1 large egg, beaten
1/4 cup Parmesan cheese, grated
1 small eggplant, sliced into 1/2-inch rounds
6 fresh mozzarella cheese slices
6 fresh basil leaves
1/4 cup tomato sauce, warmed

TIP
I like to substitute yellow squash or zucchini for the eggplant when they are in season.

Method:

1. *Fit the Tri-Grill with the upper and lower RIBBED GRILLING PLATES then set to CONTACT position.*
2. *To preheat, set the upper and lower temperature to 450°F.*
3. *Pour egg into a bowl.*
4. *Place Parmesan cheese into a separate bowl.*
5. *Dip eggplant slices into egg then roll them in Parmesan cheese until coated.*
6. *Apply nonstick spray to the Tri-Grill.*
7. *Arrange eggplant slices on the Tri-Grill; close lid.*
8. *Grill for 4-5 minutes then repeat with any remaining eggplant slices if needed.*
9. *To assemble eggplant stacks, start with an eggplant slice and layer with mozzarella cheese, basil leaves and tomato sauce.*
10. *Serve immediately.*

EGG FOO YONG

Makes 4 servings

Ingredients:

2 ounces smoked ham, diced
3 cups green cabbage, finely sliced
1 small yellow onion, diced
1 bunch green onions, chopped
1 garlic clove, minced
1 teaspoon fresh ginger, minced
2 tablespoons soy sauce
1 tablespoon sesame oil
1 teaspoon kosher salt
4 large eggs

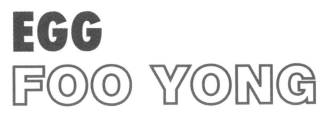

Method:

1. *Fit the Tri-Grill with the lower GRIDDLE PLATE and upper RIBBED GRILLING PLATE then set to DUAL position.*
2. *To preheat, set the lower temperature to 450°F.*
3. *In a bowl, combine all ingredients; mix well.*
4. *Apply nonstick spray to the Tri-Grill.*
5. *Place 1 1/4-cup mounds of mixture onto the GRIDDLE PLATE.*
6. *Grill for 4-5 minutes on each side then repeat with any remaining mixture.*
7. *Serve with additional soy sauce.*

HERBED
FOCACCIA

Makes 4 servings

Ingredients:

Half of a 1-pound ball of store-bought pizza dough
1 tablespoon olive oil
1/4 small yellow onion, sliced
Kosher salt and fresh pepper to taste
Pinch dried or fresh oregano

Method:

1. *Fit the Tri-Grill with the upper and lower RIBBED GRILLING PLATES then set to CONTACT position.*
2. *To preheat, set the upper and lower temperature to 350°F.*
3. *Brush olive oil all over the dough.*
4. *Stretch the dough into a rough rectangle slightly smaller than the Tri-Grill.*
5. *Carefully place dough on the Tri-Grill, stretching to the edges if necessary.*
6. *Quickly top with remaining ingredients; close lid.*
7. *Cook for 4-5 minutes or until well browned.*
8. *Remove with tongs to a cutting board, cut and serve.*

TIP

Almost all full size grocery stores in America carry fresh pizza dough. Look for it in the refrigerated case in the bakery section. If you can't find it, just ask for it. It is a huge time-saver, especially for busy working people.

THE CUBAN

Makes 2-4 servings

Ingredients:

1 large loaf Cuban bread, split and cut into 4 pieces
1/4 cup mayonnaise
1/4 cup yellow mustard
24 dill pickle slices
1 pound deli boiled ham, thinly sliced
1 pound deli pork roast, thinly sliced
1 pound deli Swiss cheese, thinly sliced

Method:

1. *Fit the Tri-Grill with the upper and lower RIBBED GRILLING PLATES then set to CONTACT position.*
2. *To preheat, set the upper and lower temperature to 350°F.*
3. *Place bread slices on a cutting board.*
4. *Spread the mayonnaise and mustard on 2 bread pieces.*
5. *Divide pickles evenly between the 2 bread pieces.*
6. *Top pickles with ham, pork and cheese.*
7. *Cover each sandwich with another bread slice.*
8. *Wrap each sandwich in parchment paper.*
9. *Place 1 sandwich on the Tri-Grill; close lid.*
10. *Press down using an oven mitt to flatten the sandwich.*
11. *Cook for 5-7 minutes or until cheese begins to melt.*
12. *Remove sandwich then repeat with remaining sandwich.*
13. *Cut into diagonal pieces before serving.*

TIP

In some Cuban sandwich shops in Florida, it is customary to make Cuban sandwiches with the addition of thin slices of hard salami as well as tomato slices. I love them both ways so try adding these ingredients next time you make this sandwich.

NEW ORLEANS
SANDWICH

Makes 1 serving

Ingredients:

1 tablespoon olive oil
1 kaiser roll, split
1 ounce Provolone cheese sliced
1 ounce mozzarella cheese, sliced
1 ounce mortadella, sliced
1 ounce capicola, sliced
1/2 cup mixed olive salad

Method:

1. *Fit the Tri-Grill with the upper and lower RIBBED GRILLING PLATES then set to CONTACT position.*
2. *To preheat, set the upper and lower temperature to 400°F.*
3. *Brush oil on the outside of the kaiser roll.*
4. *Top 1 kaiser roll half with Provolone cheese, mozzarella cheese, mortadella, capicola and olive salad.*
5. *Cover with the top kaiser roll half.*
6. *Place sandwich on the Tri-Grill; close lid.*
7. *Grill for 3-5 minutes or until golden brown and crusted.*
8. *Remove, cut and serve.*

TIP

To add some extra crunch, toast the bread slices first before assembling the sandwich then toast the entire sandwich a second time.

TURKEY & SPROUT
SANDWICH

Makes 1 serving

Ingredients:

2 teaspoons unsalted butter, softened
2 multi-grain bread slices
4 roast turkey breast slices
2 ounces cream cheese, softened
1 tablespoon sunflower seeds, toasted
1/4 cup alfalfa sprouts
Kosher salt and fresh pepper to taste
2 tablespoons Catalina dressing

Method:

1. *Fit the Tri-Grill with the upper and lower RIBBED GRILLING PLATES then set to CONTACT position.*
2. *To preheat, set the upper and lower temperature to 350°F.*
3. *Spread the butter on one side of each bread slice.*
4. *Place bread slices on the Tri-Grill; close lid.*
5. *Grill for 2-3 minutes or until very lightly toasted; remove and set aside.*
6. *Place turkey on the Tri-Grill, close lid then grill for 2-3 minutes; remove and set aside.*
7. *Spread cream cheese on one bread slice then top with sunflower seeds, turkey and sprouts.*
8. *Season with salt and pepper then drizzle the dressing over the sprouts.*
9. *Cover with other bread half and serve.*

COILED SAUSAGE

Makes 2 servings

Ingredients:

1/2 red bell pepper, julienned
1/2 green bell pepper, julienned
1/2 yellow bell pepper, julienned
1/2 large yellow onion, julienned
1 tablespoon olive oil
Kosher salt and fresh pepper to taste
Chili flakes to taste
1 pound Italian sausage
Italian rolls (optional)

Method:

1. *Fit the Tri-Grill with the upper and lower RIBBED GRILLING PLATES then set to CONTACT position.*
2. *To preheat, set the upper and lower temperature to 350°F.*
3. *Place the peppers and onions on the Tri-Grill.*
4. *Drizzle with olive oil then season with salt, pepper and chili flakes; close lid.*
5. *Cook for 4 minutes or until wilted.*
6. *Remove then place the Italian sausage on the Tri-Grill; close lid.*
7. *Cook for 6-7 minutes or until well browned and cooked through.*
8. *Remove and serve on Italian rolls if desired.*

GULF COAST PO BOY

Makes 1 serving

Ingredients:

1/2 pound large shrimp, peeled and deveined
1 tablespoon olive oil
Kosher salt and fresh pepper to taste
1 tablespoon cornmeal
1 hoagie roll, split
1 tablespoon tartar sauce
1/4 cup cabbage, shredded
1/2 carrot, shredded

RECIPES

Method:

1. *Fit the Tri-Grill with the lower GRIDDLE PLATE and upper RIBBED GRILLING PLATE then set to CONTACT position.*
2. *To preheat, set the upper and lower temperature to 400°F.*
3. *Top shrimp with oil, salt, pepper and cornmeal.*
4. *In a single layer, place the shrimp on the Tri-Grill; close lid.*
5. *Cook for 2-3 minutes or until shrimp is done; remove and set aside.*
6. *Spread the tartar sauce on the inside of the top hoagie roll half; set aside.*
7. *Top bottom hoagie roll half with cabbage, carrots and shrimp.*
8. *Season with salt and pepper then cover with top hoagie roll half.*
9. *Place hoagie on the Tri-Grill, close lid then grill for 2-3 minutes or until golden brown.*
10. *Remove and serve immediately.*

SEARED PORK KABOBS

Makes 2 servings

Ingredients:

1 pound lean pork, cut into 1-inch chunks
1/2 red bell pepper, cut into 1-inch squares
1/2 orange bell pepper, cut into 1-inch squares
1/2 green bell pepper, cut into 1-inch squares
1 tablespoon olive oil
Kosher salt and fresh pepper to taste
1 garlic clove, minced

Method:

1. *Fit the Tri-Grill with the upper and lower RIBBED GRILLING PLATES then set to CONTACT position.*
2. *To preheat, set the upper and lower temperature to 450°F.*
3. *Skewer pork chunks and bell pepper squares in an alternating manner onto two bamboo skewers.*
4. *In a bowl, stir together remaining ingredients.*
5. *Brush oil mixture onto the kabobs.*
6. *Place kabobs on the Tri-Grill; close lid.*
7. *Cook for 3-4 minutes on each side or until well browned and cooked through.*
8. *Remove and garnish as desired before serving.*

TIP

For even more flavor, brush this delicious sauce on the kabobs right after taking them off the Tri-Grill: 1 minced garlic clove, 2 teaspoons soy sauce, 2 teaspoons olive oil and a bit of fresh pepper.

FRENCH DIP

Makes 4 servings

Ingredients:

1 large yellow onion, sliced
4 tablespoons butter, divided
Kosher salt and fresh pepper to taste
2 baguettes, sliced lengthwise and halved
1 pound deli roast beef
8 Provolone cheese slices
1 cup good quality beef broth, warmed

Method:

1. *Fit the Tri-Grill with the upper and lower RIBBED GRILLING PLATES then set to CONTACT position.*
2. *To preheat, set the upper and lower temperature to 450°F.*
3. *Place onions on the Tri-Grill; dot with half of the butter.*
4. *Season with salt and pepper then close lid.*
5. *Cook for 3-4 minutes or until lightly browned.*
6. *Remove the onions; set aside.*
7. *Place baguette halves on a cutting board.*
8. *Spread remaining butter on the outside of the baguette halves.*
9. *Place onions on 4 baguette halves.*
10. *Divide the beef evenly and place on top of onions.*
11. *Season with salt and pepper then place the cheese slices over the beef.*
12. *Top each with another bread slice, butter-side up.*
13. *Place one sandwich on the Tri-Grill; close lid.*
14. *Cook for 3-4 minutes or until cheese begins to melt.*
15. *Remove and repeat with remaining sandwiches.*
16. *Serve hot with beef broth for dipping.*

TIP

To make a thinner, more flavorful sandwich, pull out some of the interior bread before assembling the sandwich.

VEGGIE SANDWICH

Makes 1 serving

Ingredients:

2 slices focaccia or other bread
2 tablespoons jarred pesto
2 tablespoons cream cheese
1 small zucchini, cut into lengthwise planks
1 small yellow squash, sliced into lengthwise planks
1 small Japanese eggplant, sliced
1 red onion, sliced into planks
2 tablespoons olive oil
Kosher salt and fresh pepper to taste

Method:

1. *Fit the Tri-Grill with the upper and lower RIBBED GRILLING PLATES then set to CONTACT position.*
2. *To preheat, set the upper and lower temperature to 450°F.*
3. *Spread pesto on one bread slice and cream cheese on the other bread slice; set aside.*
4. *In a bowl, combine zucchini, squash, eggplant and onions.*
5. *Drizzle vegetables with oil then season with salt and pepper.*
6. *Place as many vegetables as will fit onto the Tri-Grill; close lid.*
7. *Grill for 4-5 minutes or until vegetables have grill marks.*
8. *Remove and repeat with remaining vegetables.*
9. *Layer the vegetables onto a bread slice, tucking the edges under if they hang over the bread.*
10. *Top with other bread slice, dry-side up, and place on the Tri-Grill; close lid.*
11. *Grill for 4-5 minutes or until bread is toasted.*
12. *Remove and serve hot.*

REUBEN SANDWICH

Makes 1 serving

Ingredients:

2 marble rye bread slices, cut 1/2-inch thick
1 tablespoon unsalted butter, softened and divided
2 tablespoons bottled Thousand Island dressing
1/4 cup sauerkraut, drained
4 ounces corned beef, thinly sliced
1 ounce Swiss cheese, thinly sliced

Method:

1. *Fit the Tri-Grill with the upper and lower RIBBED GRILLING PLATES then set to CONTACT position.*
2. *To preheat, set the upper and lower temperature to 400°F.*
3. *Place bread slices on a cutting board.*
4. *Spread butter on one side of each bread slice.*
5. *Flip the bread slices over.*
6. *Spread the dressing on one bread slice.*
7. *Top with sauerkraut, corned beef and cheese.*
8. *Top with other bread slice, butter-side up.*
9. *Place sandwich on the Tri-Grill; close lid.*
10. *Grill for 4-5 minutes or until golden brown.*
11. *Remove, cut and serve.*

FISH TACOS

Makes 4 servings

For The Tacos:

4 mild white fish fillets, such as tilapia
2 tablespoons canola oil
1 garlic clove, minced
1 teaspoon ground cumin
1 teaspoon chili powder
Kosher salt and fresh pepper to taste

For Serving:

Corn tortillas
Salsa
Lettuce
Condiments of your choice

RECIPES

TIP

Unless your grocery store has a very well maintained
seafood department, it is often better to purchase frozen
fish fillets as they tend to be fresher.

Method:

1. *Fit the Tri-Grill with the upper and lower RIBBED GRILLING PLATES then set to CONTACT position.*
2. *To preheat, set the upper and lower temperature to 350°F.*
3. *Pat fish fillets completely dry using paper towels.*
4. *In a small bowl, combine the oil, garlic, cumin, chili powder; stir well.*
5. *Season with salt and pepper then brush mixture on both sides of the fillets.*
6. *Place 2 fillets on the Tri-Grill; close lid.*
7. *Cook for 3-4 minutes or until just done (fish will flake apart but should still be very moist when done).*
8. *Remove fish to a plate, flake apart then repeat with remaining fillets.*
9. *Serve in warm tortillas with desired toppings.*

BACON CRISPS

Makes 4 servings

Ingredients:

8 large egg roll wrappers
12 bacon slices
4 tablespoons Parmesan cheese, grated
Kosher salt and fresh pepper to taste

Method:

1. *Fit the Tri-Grill with the upper and lower RIBBED GRILLING PLATES then set to CONTACT position.*
2. *To preheat, set the upper and lower temperature to 450°F.*
3. *Lay 4 egg roll wrappers on the counter.*
4. *Top each wrapper with 3 bacon slices, trimming them to cover the wrappers completely.*
5. *Sprinkle with Parmesan cheese then season with salt and pepper.*
6. *Top each with another egg roll wrapper.*
7. *Place 1 crisp on the Tri-Grill; close lid.*
8. *Cook for 4-5 minutes or until well browned and crispy.*
9. *Remove then place on paper towels to drain.*
10. *Repeat with remaining crisps.*
11. *Cut into desired shape using a knife or pizza wheel.*
12. *Serve warm.*

CHICKEN QUESADILLA

Makes 2 servings

Ingredients:

2 flour tortillas
1/4 cup bottled BBQ sauce
1/2 cup leftover rotisserie chicken, shredded
1/4 cup red onions, thinly sliced
1 cup Monterrey Jack cheese, shredded
1/2 jalapeño pepper, seeded and sliced
2 tablespoons cilantro, chopped

Method:

1. *Fit the Tri-Grill with the lower GRIDDLE PLATE and upper RIBBED GRILLING PLATE then set to CONTACT position.*
2. *To preheat, set the upper and lower temperature to 400°F.*
3. *Place one tortilla on a cutting board and spread with BBQ sauce.*
4. *Top evenly with chicken, red onions, cheese and jalapeño peppers.*
5. *Cover with the other tortilla.*
6. *Apply nonstick spray to the Tri-Grill.*
7. *Place the quesadilla on the Tri-Grill; close lid.*
8. *Cook for 4-5 minutes or until cheese is melted.*
9. *Transfer quesadilla to a cutting board.*
10. *Cut into wedges, top with cilantro and serve.*

PATTY
MELTS

Makes 2 servings

Ingredients:

1 pound lean ground beef
1 tablespoon bottled steak sauce
1 teaspoon onion powder
Kosher salt and fresh pepper to taste
4 aged Cheddar cheese slices

Method:

1. *Fit the Tri-Grill with the upper and lower RIBBED GRILLING PLATES then set to CONTACT position.*
2. *To preheat, set the upper and lower temperature to 450°F.*
3. *In a mixing bowl, combine the beef, steak sauce, onion powder, salt and pepper.*
4. *Form mixture into two equal patties then season exterior with additional salt and pepper.*
5. *Place patties on the Tri-Grill; close lid.*
6. *Cook for 4 minutes or until desired doneness.*
7. *Raise the lid then lay two slices of cheese on top of each patty.*
8. *Set Tri-Grill to FIXED position.*
9. *Leave patties on the Tri-Grill, lower the lid and cook for an additional 30 seconds or until cheese is melted.*
10. *Remove and garnish as desired before serving.*

TIP

You can jazz up these patties by rolling the meat in crushed up potato chips before placing them on the Tri-Grill. The contrast of hot beef, melted cheese and crunchy chips is irresistible.

ALLOW PLATES TO COOL BLF. RE REMOVING

CROQUE MONSIEUR

Makes 2 sandwiches

Ingredients:

4 firm white bread slices
2 teaspoons unsalted butter
2 tablespoons apricot jam
8 smoked deli ham slices
1 tomato, sliced
1 cup gruyere or Swiss cheese, diced
1/3 cup mayonnaise
2 teaspoons bottled horseradish
1 tablespoon Dijon mustard

Method:

1. *Fit the Tri-Grill with the lower GRIDDLE PLATE and upper RIBBED GRILLING PLATE then set to FIXED position.*
2. *To preheat, set the upper and lower temperature to 450°F.*
3. *Place bread slices on a cutting board.*
4. *Spread butter on 1 side of each bread slice.*
5. *Flip slices over then spread jam on 2 slices.*
6. *Top each jam slice with ham and tomatoes.*
7. *Cover each with another bread slice, butter-side up.*
8. *In a bowl, combine remaining ingredients.*
9. *Spread cheese mixture on top of each sandwich.*
10. *Place sandwiches on the Tri-Grill; lower lid.*
11. *Cook sandwiches for 5-7 minutes or until bottom bread is brown and cheese is bubbly.*
12. *Remove and serve immediately.*

BREAKFAST HASH

Makes 3-4 servings

Ingredients:

2 tablespoons unsalted butter
1 large yellow onion, diced
4 cups leftover boiled potatoes, cubed
2 cups leftover corned beef, cubed
1/4 green bell pepper, diced
Kosher salt and fresh pepper to taste
Fresh parsley, chopped
Ketchup (optional)

Method:

1. *Fit the Tri-Grill with the lower GRIDDLE PLATE and upper RIBBED GRILLING PLATE then set to DUAL position.*
2. *To preheat, set the lower temperature to 400°F.*
3. *Place the butter on the GRIDDLE PLATE.*
4. *When butter sizzles, add the onions and stir until they begin to brown.*
5. *Add the potatoes; cook for 7-10 minutes, stirring occasionally.*
6. *Add corned beef, bell peppers, salt and pepper, let cook until a crust forms.*
7. *Flip and cook until well browned on the other side.*
8. *Top with parsley and serve with ketchup if desired.*

SEARED TUNA

Makes 2 servings

For The Tuna:

2 (5 ounces each) ahi tuna steaks
2 teaspoons canola oil
2 teaspoons sesame seeds
Kosher salt and fresh pepper

For The Dipping Sauce:

2 scallions, thinly sliced
1 small garlic clove, minced
1/2 teaspoon fresh ginger, minced
1 teaspoon dark sesame oil
2 teaspoons honey
2 teaspoons soy sauce
1/2 teaspoon sriracha or hot sauce
1 teaspoon fresh lime juice
1 tablespoon cashew or peanut butter

Method:

1. *Fit the Tri-Grill with the lower GRIDDLE plate and upper RIBBED GRILLING PLATE then set to DUAL position.*
2. *To preheat, set the lower temperature to 450°F.*
3. *Brush tuna with oil then sprinkle with sesame seeds, salt and pepper.*
4. *Place tuna on Tri-Grill and grill each side for 1 minute.*
5. *Using tongs, cook for 30 seconds on all edges.*
6. *Remove at once for a rare center or cook longer if desired; do not overcook.*
7. *In a bowl, combine dipping sauce ingredients; whisk until smooth and serve as a dipping sauce with the tuna.*

GRILLED WHOLE CHICKEN

Makes 3-4 servings

Ingredients:
1 whole chicken, backbone removed
2 tablespoons olive oil
Kosher salt and fresh pepper to taste
3 tablespoons green onions, chopped

Method:
1. *Fit the Tri-Grill with the lower GRIDDLE PLATE and upper RIBBED GRILLING PLATE then set to CONTACT position.*
2. *To preheat, set the upper and lower temperature to 450°F.*
3. *Make a slit in the bottom of the breast bone and butterfly the chicken.*
4. *Rub olive oil over the entire chicken.*
5. *Season with salt and pepper.*
6. *Place chicken on the Tri-Grill; close lid.*
7. *Cook for 12-15 minutes or until internal temperature registers 165°F on a meat thermometer.*
8. *Garnish with green onions and serve.*

KC STRIP STEAK

Makes 1 serving

For The Steak:
2 teaspoons olive oil
1 (10-ounce) strip loin steak
Kosher salt and fresh pepper to taste
6 bell pepper strips

For The Dipping Sauce:
2 tablespoons Worcestershire sauce
2 tablespoons mayonnaise

Method:

1. *Fit the Tri-Grill with the upper and lower RIBBED GRILLING PLATES then set to CONTACT position.*
2. *To preheat, set the upper and lower temperature to 450°F.*
3. *Brush oil on both sides of steak and peppers.*
4. *Season to taste with salt and pepper on both sides.*
5. *Place steak and peppers on the Tri-Grill; close lid.*
6. *Grill for 2-4 minutes then rotate steak by a quarter turn to achieve the criss-cross grill marks; continue to grill for another 2-4 minutes or until desired doneness.*
7. *Remove and let rest for 5 minutes before slicing.*
8. *In a small bowl, stir together the dipping sauce ingredients.*
9. *Garnish as desired then serve with the dipping sauce on the side.*

To avoid overcooking an expensive steak, I recommend investing in an instant read meat thermometer. Pushing the probe into the side wall of the steak rather than inserting into the top will allow you to take a more accurate temperature measurement.

RECIPES

ITALIAN GRILLED CHEESE SANDWICH

Makes 2 servings

Ingredients:

4 crusty white bread slices, cut 1/2-inch thick
2 tablespoons unsalted butter, divided
1 tablespoon jarred pesto
4 Provolone cheese slices

Method:

1. *Fit the Tri-Grill with the upper and lower RIBBED GRILLING PLATES then set to CONTACT position.*
2. *To preheat, set the upper and lower temperature to 400°F.*
3. *Place bread slices on a cutting board and spread 1/2 tablespoon of butter on one side of each bread slice.*
4. *Flip bread slices over and spread 1/2 tablespoon pesto on two bread slices.*
5. *Place 2 slices of cheese on top of each pesto slice.*
6. *Top each with another bread slice, butter-side up.*
7. *Place sandwiches on the Tri-Grill; close lid.*
8. *Grill for 3-5 minutes or until bread is golden brown and cheese is melted.*
9. *Remove, cut and serve.*

WHOLE GRAIN
BLTA

Makes 1 serving

Ingredients:

2 tablespoons unsalted butter, divided
2 slices 7 grain bread, cut 1/2-inch thick
4 bacon slices
1 tablespoon mayonnaise
2 large pieces iceberg lettuce
1/4 ripe avocado, cut 1/4-inch thick
2 slices vine ripe tomatoes, cut 1/4-inch thick
Kosher salt and fresh pepper to taste

Method:

1. *Fit the Tri-Grill with the upper and lower RIBBED GRILLING PLATES then set to CONTACT position.*
2. *To preheat, set the upper and lower temperature to 400°F.*
3. *Spread 1/2 tablespoon butter on both sides of each bread slice.*
4. *Place bread slices on the Tri-Grill; close lid.*
5. *Grill for 2-3 minutes or until bread is golden brown.*
6. *Remove bread slices and set aside.*
7. *Place the bacon on the Tri-Grill; close lid.*
8. *Grill for 3-4 minutes or until bacon is cooked to desired doneness.*
9. *Transfer bacon onto paper towels to drain; let cool for 2 minutes.*
10. *Spread the mayonnaise on one bread slice.*
11. *Top with lettuce, avocado, tomatoes, and bacon.*
12. *Season with salt and pepper.*
13. *Top with other bread slice, cut and serve.*

TURKEY BURGERS

Makes 2 servings

For The Burgers:

6 ounces lean ground turkey
2 tablespoons ricotta cheese
1 tablespoon yellow onions, minced
1 tablespoon celery, minced
1/4 teaspoon dried sage
Kosher salt and pepper to taste

For Serving:

Soft buns
Bib lettuce
Mayonnaise
Cranberry sauce

Method:

1. *Fit the Tri-Grill with the upper and lower RIBBED GRILLING PLATES then set to CONTACT position.*

2. *To preheat, set the upper and lower temperature to 450°F.*

3. *In a bowl, combine all burger ingredients.*

4. *Form mixture into 2 patties.*

5. *Place patties on the Tri-Grill; close lid.*

6. *Grill for 5 minutes or until cooked through.*

7. *Remove and serve on buns with lettuce, mayonnaise and cranberry sauce.*

PESTO SHRIMP
KABOBS

Makes 1-2 servings

For The Shrimp:
8 large shrimp, peeled, deveined and thawed
Kosher salt and fresh pepper to taste

For The Pesto:
3 garlic cloves
3 tablespoons olive oil
3 tablespoons pine nuts
3 tablespoons Parmesan Cheese
3 handful fresh basil leaves

Method:
1. *Fit the Tri-Grill with the upper and lower RIBBED GRILLING PLATES then set to CONTACT position.*
2. *To preheat, set the upper and lower temperature to 450°F.*
3. *Dry the shrimp on a kitchen towel then lay them flat in a "C" shape onto a cutting board.*
4. *Skewer shrimp onto 2 bamboo skewers.*
5. *Combine all pesto ingredients in a blender; pulse to combine.*
6. *Brush skewers with pesto then season with salt and pepper.*
7. *Place skewers on the Tri-Grill; close lid.*
8. *Cook for 2-3 minutes or until shrimp is done.*
9. *Remove and serve with additional pesto for dipping.*

EGGS IN A NEST

Makes 2 servings

Ingredients:

2 tablespoons unsalted butter
2 bread slices of your choice, cut 1 1/2-inch thick
2 large eggs
Kosher salt and fresh pepper to taste

Method:

1. Fit the Tri-Grill with the lower GRIDDLE PLATE and upper RIBBED GRILLING PLATE then set to CONTACT position.
2. To preheat, set the upper and lower temperature to 450°F.
3. Spread the butter on both sides of each bread slice.
4. Make a hole in the center of each bread slice, making sure not to go all the way through.
5. Place bread slices on the Tri-Grill and crack an egg into each hole; close lid.
6. Cook for 4-5 minutes or until bread is golden brown and eggs are cooked to desired doneness.
7. Remove then season with salt and pepper.
8. Serve immediately.

FRENCH TOAST ON A STICK

Makes 2 servings

Ingredients:

1 French baguette, 12-inches long
6 large eggs
1/4 cup milk
Pinch of kosher salt

Method:

1. *Fit the Tri-Grill with the lower GRIDDLE PLATE and upper RIBBED GRILLING PLATE then set to DUAL position.*
2. *To preheat, set the lower temperature to 350°F.*
3. *Cut off the ends from the baguette then cut in half lengthwise.*
4. *Cut each baguette half into two 6-inch long pieces.*
5. *Run a bamboo skewer through each baguette piece.*
6. *In a bowl, whisk together the eggs, milk and salt.*
7. *Pour the egg mixture to a 9x9-inch pan.*
8. *Dip bread skewers in egg mixture, covering all sides.*
9. *Place 2 skewers on the Tri-Grill.*
10. *Cook for 2-3 minutes on each side or until golden brown.*
11. *Remove then repeat with remaining skewers.*
12. *Remove and serve as desired.*

CHIPOTLE
FLANK STEAK

Makes 4 servings

Ingredients:

1 tablespoon chipotle chili powder
1 tablespoon paprika
Kosher salt and pepper to taste
1 tablespoon canola oil
2 pounds flank steak, trimmed

Method:

1. *Fit the Tri-Grill with the upper and lower RIBBED GRILLING PLATES then set to CONTACT position.*
2. *To preheat, set the lower temperature to 450°F.*
3. *In a bowl, combine chipotle chili powder, paprika, salt and pepper; mix well.*
4. *Pat the flank steak dry using paper towels.*
5. *Brush steak with oil then sprinkle chipotle mixture on both sides of the steak.*
6. *Place the steak on the Tri-Grill; close lid.*
7. *Cook for 3-4 minutes or until desired doneness.*
8. *Remove to a cutting board and let rest for 3-4 minutes.*
9. *Cut across the grain into thin slices, garnish as desired and serve.*

TIP
Do not cook this meat
past medium or it will get tough.

TEX MEX
STREET CORN

Makes 4 servings

For The Corn:
4 ears of fresh corn

For Topping:
Mayonnaise to taste
Chipotle powder to taste
Queso fresco cheese, shredded
Parmesan cheese to taste
Lime wedges
Cilantro, chopped

Method:

1. *Fit the Tri-Grill with the upper and lower RIBBED GRILLING PLATES then set to DUAL position.*
2. *Place the corn on the Tri-Grill and cook for a total of 20 minutes, turning each corn by 1/4 turn every 5 minutes.*
3. *While corn is cooking, place each topping ingredient in separate bowl.*
4. *When corn is done, brush with desired amount of mayonnaise.*
5. *Sprinkle desired amount of chipotle powder and cheese over the corn.*
6. *Squeeze lime juice onto the corn and garnish with cilantro before serving.*

SOUTH OF THE BORDER PIZZA

Makes 1 serving

Ingredients:

1/4 cup refried beans
2 corn tortillas or 1 flour tortilla
1/4 cup leftover rotisserie chicken, shredded
2 tablespoons salsa
1/2 jalapeño pepper, seeded and sliced
1/3 cup Monterey Jack cheese, shredded
Kosher salt and fresh pepper to taste
Fresh cilantro, chopped

Method:

1. *Fit the Tri-Grill with the lower GRIDDLE PLATE and upper RIBBED GRILLING PLATE then set to FIXED position.*
2. *To preheat, set the upper and lower temperature to 450°F.*
3. *Spread the refried beans over the tortillas.*
4. *Top with chicken, salsa, jalapeño peppers and cheese.*
5. *Season with salt and pepper.*
6. *Place pizza on the Tri-Grill; lower lid.*
7. *Cook for 8-10 minutes or until tortilla is crispy and cheese is melted.*
8. *Garnish with cilantro and serve.*

CORN CAKES

Makes 4 servings

Ingredients:

2 1/2 cups fresh or frozen (thawed) corn kernels
1 1/2 cups panko breadcrumbs
1/3 cup all purpose flour
1/4 cup Parmesan cheese, grated
3 large eggs
1/4 cup red bell peppers, diced
2 green onions, finely sliced
Kosher salt and fresh pepper to taste
4 tablespoons unsalted butter, melted

Method:

1. *Fit the Tri-Grill with the lower GRIDDLE PLATE and upper RIBBED GRILLING PLATE then set to DUAL position.*
2. *To preheat, set the lower temperature to 450°F.*
3. *In a bowl, combine the corn, panko, flour, cheese, eggs, bell peppers, green onions, salt and pepper; whisk well.*
4. *Drizzle melted butter onto the GRIDDLE PLATE.*
5. *Drop batter by 2 tablespoons onto the GRIDDLE PLATE.*
6. *Using a spatula, gently pat the batter into circles and cook for 3 minutes or until brown.*
7. *Flip and cook for an additional 3 minutes.*
8. *Remove and repeat with remaining batter.*
9. *Serve as desired.*

STUFFED BURGERS

Makes 2 servings

For The Burgers:

1 1/2 pounds ground beef chuck
4 ounces blue cheese, crumbled
Kosher salt and fresh pepper to taste

For Serving:

Soft buns
Tomato slices
Red onion slices
Lettuce leaves
Condiments of your choice

Method:

1. *Fit the Tri-Grill with the upper and lower RIBBED GRILLING PLATES then set to CONTACT position.*
2. *To preheat, set the upper and lower temperature to 450°F.*
3. *On a plastic wrap-covered counter, divide the meat into 4 portions.*
4. *Shape each portion into a 5-inch patty.*
5. *Divide the blue cheese evenly onto 2 of the patties, keeping the edges clean.*
6. *Lay another patty over each blue cheese patty then press all around the edges to seal.*
7. *Season burgers with salt and pepper.*
8. *Place patties on the Tri-Grill; close lid.*
9. *Cook for 4-5 minutes or until desired doneness.*
10. *Remove and place on buns.*
11. *Add desired toppings and condiments before serving.*

DESSERT PIZZA

Makes 4 servings

Ingredients:
1 pound store-bought pizza dough ball, divided
2 tablespoons unsalted butter, melted
1/2 cup strawberry jam, warmed until fluid
1 cup semi-sweet chocolate chips
1 cup shredded coconut
1 cup raspberries
1 cup kiwi, diced
1 cup blueberries

Method:
1. *Fit the Tri-Grill with the lower GRIDDLE PLATE and upper RIBBED GRILLING PLATE then set to CONTACT position.*
2. *To preheat, set the lower temperature to 300°F.*
3. *Stretch both pizza dough balls into rough 8-inch circles.*
4. *Brush both sides of the dough with melted butter.*
5. *Place a dough circle on the Tri-Grill; close lid.*
6. *Cook for 4-5 minutes or until desired doneness; repeat with other dough circle.*
7. *Remove pizza crusts to a cutting board then quickly spread with the jam.*
8. *Scatter the chocolate over the crusts (the heat from the dough will melt the chocolate).*
9. *Top with remaining ingredients, cut into wedges and serve.*

TIP
The refrigerated dough that is packaged in a tube and available in the dairy section of your grocery store is perfect for this pizza.

TRI-GRILL
PINEAPPLE

Makes 2 servings

Ingredients:

4 fresh pineapple slices, cut 1/2-inch thick, core removed
Pinch of kosher salt
2 tablespoons granulated sugar
2 small scoops raspberry sorbet
2 small mint leaves

For The Raspberry Coulis:

1 bag (12 ounces) frozen raspberries, thawed
2/3 cup granulated sugar

Method:

1. *Fit the Tri-Grill with the upper and lower RIBBED GRILLING PLATES then set to CONTACT position.*
2. *To preheat, set the upper and lower temperature to 400°F.*
3. *Place pineapple slices on the Tri-Grill.*
4. *Sprinkle pineapple slices with salt then close lid.*
5. *Grill for 2-3 minutes.*
6. *Remove then sprinkle with sugar.*
7. *In a blender, blend all raspberry coulis ingredients until very smooth; strain through a fine strainer to remove seeds if desired.*
8. *Pour raspberry coulis onto each serving plate.*
9. *Place 2 pineapple slices onto each plate.*
10. *Top each with a scoop of sorbet and mint leaf before serving.*

RASPBERRY RICOTTA SANDWICHES

Makes 2 servings

For The Sandwiches:
2 French bread slices, cut diagonally 1-inch thick
2 teaspoons unsalted butter, softened
1 cup fresh raspberries
2 teaspoons honey

For The Sweet Ricotta Spread:
3/4 cup whole milk ricotta cheese
1/4 cup sour cream
2 tablespoons granulated sugar
1/2 teaspoon fresh lemon juice

Method:

1. *Fit the Tri-Grill with the upper and lower RIBBED GRILLING PLATES then set to CONTACT position.*
2. *To preheat, set the upper and lower temperature to 350°F.*
3. *Spread butter on both sides of the bread slices.*
4. *Apply nonstick spray to the Tri-Grill.*
5. *Place bread slices on the Tri-Grill; close lid.*
6. *Grill for 3-4 minutes.*
7. *To make the sweet ricotta spread, combine all spread ingredients in a bowl; mix well.*
8. *Top each bread slice with ricotta spread, raspberries and honey.*
9. *Serve immediately.*

ISLAND CHICKEN BURGERS

Makes 4 servings

For The Burgers:

1 pound ground chicken
1/4 cup dried pineapple, finely chopped
Kosher salt and fresh pepper to taste
1 cup shredded dry coconut
1 cup panko breadcrumbs
2 tablespoons canola oil

For Serving:

Soft buns
Condiments of your choice

Method:

1. Fit the Tri-Grill with the upper and lower RIBBED GRILLING PLATES then set to CONTACT position.
2. To preheat, set the upper and lower temperature to 450°F.
3. In a mixing bowl, combine the chicken, pineapple, salt and pepper.
4. Mix well then form into four 4-inch round patties.
5. In a shallow bowl, combine the dry coconut and panko.
6. Press each patty evenly into the coconut-panko mixture.
7. Lightly brush Tri-Grill with oil.
8. Place 2 patties on the Tri-Grill; close lid.
9. Cook for 4-5 minutes or until well browned and internal temperature reaches 165°F on a meat thermometer.
10. Remove and repeat with remaining patties.
11. Serve on buns with condiments of your choice.

ROSEMARY SKEWERED CHICKEN

Makes 4 servings

For The Herb Mixture:

3 tablespoons canola oil
8 garlic cloves, crushed
2 tablespoons dried oregano
2 teaspoons fresh thyme, finely chopped
1 tablespoon lemon juice
Kosher salt and pepper to taste

For The Chicken:

3 boneless, skinless chicken breasts, cut into 1½-inch cubes
8 rosemary sprigs
1/2 cup feta cheese, crumbled
8 fresh mint leaves, julienned

Method:

1. *Fit the Tri-Grill with the upper and lower RIBBED GRILLING PLATES then set to CONTACT position.*
2. *To preheat, set the upper and lower temperature to 450°F.*
3. *In a bowl, combine all herb mixture ingredients; mix well.*
4. *Thread 4-5 chicken cubes on each rosemary sprig.*
5. *Brush each kabob with the herb mixture.*
6. *Place kabobs on the Tri-Grill; close lid.*
7. *Cook for 3-4 minutes or until internal temperature reaches 165°F on a meat thermometer.*
8. *Serve chicken garnished with feta cheese and mint leaves.*

TIP
You can also make these kabobs with
cubed up pork chops instead of chicken.

LAMB CHOPS

Makes 2 servings

Ingredients:

6 lamb chops, Frenched
1/2 cup jarred pesto
Kosher salt and fresh pepper to taste

Method:

1. *Fit the Tri-Grill with the upper and lower RIBBED GRILLING PLATES then set to CONTACT position.*
2. *To preheat, set the upper and lower temperature to 450°F.*
3. *Brush both sides of the lamb chops with pesto.*
4. *Season with salt and pepper.*
5. *Place lamb chops on the Tri-Grill; close lid.*
6. *Cook for 3-5 minutes or until desired doneness.*
7. *Remove and serve with additional pesto.*

TIP
You can ask your butcher to clean the rack of lamb bones for you. This is called "Frenching" the bones.

MUSHROOM BURGERS

Makes 2 servings

Ingredients:

8 ounces fresh cremini mushrooms, chopped
8 ounces button mushrooms, sliced
1 tablespoon olive oil
2 garlic cloves, minced
1 teaspoon unsalted butter
1 teaspoon kosher salt
1/2 teaspoon freshly ground pepper
2 tablespoons Parmesan cheese, grated
1/2 bunch green onions, chopped
1/3 cup panko breadcrumbs
Soft rolls
Lettuce (optional)
Mayonnaise

Method:

1. *In a sauté pan on the stovetop over medium-high heat, add the mushrooms and oil.*
2. *Add the garlic, butter, salt and pepper; stir well.*
3. *Cook for 10 minutes, stirring often until the mushrooms are browned, the bottom of the pan is coated with brown bits and all of the moisture has evaporated.*
4. *Remove to a bowl then add the cheese, green onions and breadcrumbs; mix well.*
5. *Form mixture into 2 patties; refrigerate until firm.*
6. *Fit the Tri-Grill with the upper and lower RIBBED GRILLING PLATES then set to CONTACT position.*
7. *Apply nonstick spray to the Tri-Grill then place patties on the Tri-Grill; close lid.*
8. *Cook for 5 minutes or until browned.*
9. *Remove and serve on soft rolls with mayonnaise and lettuce if desired.*

VEGGIE KABOBS

Makes 2 servings

Ingredients:

8 small Campari tomatoes
2 zucchini, cut into 1-inch coins
Olive oil
Kosher salt and fresh pepper to taste

Method:

1. *Fit the Tri-Grill with the upper and lower RIBBED GRILLING PLATES then set to CONTACT position.*
2. *To preheat, set the upper and lower temperature to 450°F.*
3. *Place the tomatoes and zucchini in an alternating manner onto two skewers.*
4. *Brush skewers with olive oil.*
5. *Season skewers with salt and pepper.*
6. *Place skewers on the Tri-Grill; close lid.*
7. *Grill for 3-4 minutes.*
8. *Remove and serve immediately.*

POTATO CRISPS

Makes 1-2 servings

Ingredients:

2 medium Russet potatoes, peeled, shredded then squeezed dry
2 tablespoons unsalted butter, melted
Kosher salt and fresh pepper to taste

Method:

1. *Fit the Tri-Grill with the lower GRIDDLE PLATE and upper RIBBED GRILLING PLATE then set to DUAL position.*
2. *To preheat, set the lower temperature to 450°F.*
3. *Divide the potatoes into 3 mounds on the Tri-Grill.*
4. *Drizzle with butter then season with salt and pepper.*
5. *Cook for 7 minutes on each side or until well browned.*
6. *Remove and serve hot with desired toppings.*

TIP

Make sure to squeeze out all of the water from the potatoes or they will not get crispy. This recipe also works well with sweet potatoes.

FRENCH

TOAST

Makes 4 servings

For The French Toast:
2 cups heavy cream
6 eggs, beaten
1 loaf challah or brioche bread, thickly sliced

For Serving:
Butter
Maple syrup
Powdered sugar

Method:

1. *Fit the Tri-Grill with the lower GRIDDLE PLATE and upper RIBBED GRILLING PLATE then set to DUAL position.*
2. *To preheat, set the lower temperature to 350°F.*
3. *Beat the cream and eggs together in a bowl.*
4. *Dip the bread slices into the egg mixture on both sides.*
5. *Place the bread slices on the Tri-Grill.*
6. *Cook 3-4 minutes on each side or until golden brown.*
7. *Remove then repeat with remaining bread.*
8. *Serve with butter, syrup and powdered sugar.*

EGGS IN A BOAT

Makes 4 servings

Ingredients:

1 1/2 tablespoons unsalted butter, melted
4 baguette slices, cut 1/2-inch thick
4 tablespoons heavy cream, divided
4 tablespoons Parmesan cheese, shredded
4 large eggs
Chives, chopped
Kosher salt and fresh pepper to taste

Method:

1. *Fit the Tri-Grill with the upper and lower RIBBED GRILLING PLATES then set to CONTACT position.*
2. *To preheat, set the upper temperature to 450°F and lower temperature to 350°F.*
3. *Brush the butter on the inside of 4 ramekins.*
4. *Place 1 baguette slice into each ramekin.*
5. *Pour 1 tablespoon heavy cream into each ramekin.*
6. *Sprinkle 1 tablespoon cheese into each ramekin.*
7. *Crack 1 egg into each ramekin.*
8. *Place 2 ramekins on the Tri-Grill; slowly lower the lid until it rests on the ramekins.*
9. *Cook for 5-6 minutes or until eggs are cooked to desired doneness.*
10. *Remove using pot holders then repeat with remaining ramekins.*
11. *Sprinkle with chives, season with salt and pepper then garnish as desired before serving.*

CRAB CAKES

Makes 2 cakes

Ingredients:

1 bread slice, crusts removed, torn into small pieces
8 ounces jumbo lump fresh crab meat
1 green onion, minced
1 tablespoon bell peppers, minced
1 tablespoon mayonnaise
1/2 teaspoon kosher salt
2 teaspoons olive oil

Method:

1. *In a bowl, combine all ingredients, except oil.*
2. *Form mixture into 2 equally sized patties.*
3. *Refrigerate patties for 20 minutes.*
4. *Fit the Tri-Grill with the upper and lower RIBBED GRILLING PLATES then set to CONTACT position.*
5. *To preheat, set the upper and lower temperature to 450°F.*
6. *Lightly brush olive oil on both RIBBED GRILLING PLATES.*
7. *Place the crab cakes on the Tri-Grill; close lid.*
8. *Cook for 3-4 minutes.*
9. *Remove and serve.*

TIP

Using fresh and moist breadcrumbs ensures moist crab cakes. Using dry breadcrumbs or panko will soak up the moisture, making these crab cakes heavy and dry.

BISON BURGERS

Makes 2 servings

Ingredients:
8 ounces ground bison
Kosher salt and fresh pepper to taste
2 soft buns

Method:
1. *Fit the Tri-Grill with the upper and lower RIBBED GRILLING PLATES then set to CONTACT position.*
2. *To preheat, set the upper and lower temperature to 350°F.*
3. *Divide ground bison and shape into 2 equally sized patties; season with salt and pepper.*
4. *Apply nonstick spray to the Tri-Grill.*
5. *Place patties on the Tri-Grill; close lid.*
6. *Cook for 3-4 minutes or until desired doneness; do not overcook.*
7. *Serve on buns with your favorite condiments.*

TIP
You can buy 4 ounce individually wrapped bison burgers ready-to-cook from Body By Bison (see source page 106).

GOOEY S'MORES

Makes 2 servings

Ingredients:

4 slices pound cake, cut 3/4-inch thick
2 chocolate bars, broken in half
8 large marshmallows

Method:

1. Fit the Tri-Grill with the lower GRIDDLE PLATE and upper RIBBED GRILLING PLATE then set to CONTACT position.
2. To preheat, set the upper and lower temperature to 300°F.
3. Apply nonstick spray to one side of each slice of pound cake.
4. Place 2 cake slices, sprayed-side down on a cutting board.
5. Top each slice with a piece of chocolate then top each with 4 marshmallows.
6. Top marshmallows with another piece of chocolate.
7. Top each S'mores with a slice of cake, sprayed-side up.
8. Place S'mores on the Tri-Grill; close lid.
9. Grill for 3-5 minutes or until chocolate is melted.
10. Serve immediately.

TIP

You can use this same recipe with even slices of chocolate cake for an even more decadent treat.

STRAWBERRY SHORTCAKES

Makes 4 servings

For The Biscuit Dough:
1 1/2 cups all purpose flour
1 1/2 teaspoons baking powder
1/2 teaspoon kosher salt
1 tablespoon granulated sugar
1 1/2 cups heavy cream

For The Berries:
2 cups fresh strawberries, sliced
3 tablespoons granulated sugar

For Assembly:
Sweetened whipped cream to taste
Powdered sugar, for serving

Method:

1. *Fit the Tri-Grill with the lower GRIDDLE PLATE and upper RIBBED GRILLING PLATE then set to DUAL position.*

2. *To preheat, set the lower temperature to 300°F.*

3. *In a bowl, stir together all biscuit dough ingredients using a fork.*

4. *Stir vigorously until a dough forms that cleans the sides of the bowl.*

5. *Using a small ice cream scoop, divide the dough into 8 mounds.*

6. *Using the palm of your hand, flatten slightly to 1/3-inch thick.*

7. *Place dough on the Tri-Grill and cook for 8 minutes on each side or until golden brown.*

8. *While the biscuits are cooking, stir together the strawberries and sugar in a bowl; let stand to pull some of the juices out of the berries.*

9. *Place 4 of the biscuits onto 4 plates.*

10. *Top each biscuit with some berries and whipped cream then repeat to make a second layer.*

11. *Dust with powdered sugar and serve immediately.*

PEANUT BUTTER & BANANA
PITA

Makes 1-2 servings

Ingredients:

1 pita bread, cut in half
4 tablespoons peanut butter
2 bananas, sliced

RECIPES

Method:

1. *Fit the Tri-Grill with the upper and lower RIBBED GRILLING PLATES then set to CONTACT position.*

2. *To preheat, set the upper and lower temperature to 400°F.*

3. *Spread 2 tablespoons peanut butter inside each pita bread half.*

4. *Place banana slices into each pita half.*

5. *Spray both sides of the pita halves with nonstick cooking spray.*

6. *Place pitas on the Tri-Grill; close lid.*

7. *Grill for 4-5 minutes or until pita is crispy.*

8. *Remove and serve immediately.*

CHOCOLATE MARSHMALLOW PANINI

Makes 1 serving

Ingredients:

2 challah bread slices, cut 3/4-inch thick
1 tablespoon unsalted butter, softened and divided
2 tablespoons chocolate-hazelnut spread
2 tablespoons marshmallow fluff

Method:

1. *Fit the Tri-Grill with the upper and lower RIBBED GRILLING PLATES then set to CONTACT position.*
2. *To preheat, set the upper and lower temperature to 400°F.*
3. *Place bread slices on a cutting board.*
4. *Spread the butter on one side of each bread slice.*
5. *Flip the bread slices over.*
6. *Spread the chocolate-hazelnut spread on one bread slice and marshmallow fluff on the other bread slice.*
7. *Put the two bread slices together.*
8. *Place panini on the Tri-Grill; close lid.*
9. *Grill for 3-5 minutes or until golden brown.*
10. *Remove and serve immediately.*

LEMON CREPE STACK

Makes 4-6 servings

Ingredients:

1 prepared recipe Basic Crepes (see page 84)
1 1/2 cups heavy whipping cream
1/4 cup granulated sugar
1 jar (15 oz.) lemon curd
1 of each segmented orange, blood orange and grapefruit

Method:

1. *In a stand mixer fitted with the whisk attachment, combine the heavy whipping cream and sugar.*
2. *Whip on medium-high speed until semi-stiff peaks form; remove from the mixer.*
3. *Place a crepe onto a decorative cake plate.*
4. *Top crepe with a spoonful of lemon curd and spread to the edges.*
5. *Top with a crepe and spread a spoonful of whipped cream mixture to the edges.*
6. *Repeat until all crepes are filled, leaving the top crepe without a topping.*
7. *Arrange the citrus segments on top of the cake.*
8. *Refrigerate for 1 hour.*
9. *Slice into wedges and serve.*

COCONUT CHICKEN

Makes 2 servings

Ingredients:

2 boneless, skinless chicken breasts
1/4 cup panko breadcrumbs
1 tablespoon fresh parsley, chopped
1/4 cup shredded coconut
1 large egg white, beaten
Kosher salt and fresh pepper to taste
1/4 cup sweetened cream of coconut
Lime wedges

Method:

1. *Fit the Tri-Grill with the lower GRIDDLE PLATE and upper RIBBED GRILLING PLATE then set to CONTACT position.*
2. *To preheat, set the upper and lower temperature to 350°F.*
3. *On a piece of plastic wrap, pound chicken breasts with a meat mallet to even out the thickness.*
4. *On a plate combine the panko, parsley and coconut.*
5. *Pour the egg white into a small bowl.*
6. *Season chicken with salt and pepper.*
7. *Dip each chicken breast in egg white then roll in coconut mixture.*
8. *Place chicken on the Tri-Grill; close lid.*
9. *Cook for 7 minutes or until internal temperature reaches 165°F on a meat thermometer.*
10. *Remove then drizzle cream of coconut over the chicken.*
11. *Serve with lime wedges.*

EASY ITALIAN
PANINI

Makes 1 serving

Ingredients:

2 Italian bread slices, cut 1/2-inch thick
1 tablespoon unsalted butter, divided
1/2 tablespoon mayonnaise
2 capicola slices, cut thin
2 mortadella slices, cut thin
2 salami slices, cut thin
2 Provolone cheese slices, cut thin

Method:

1. *Fit the Tri-Grill with the upper and lower RIBBED GRILLING PLATES then set to CONTACT position.*

2. *To preheat, set the upper and lower temperature to 450°F.*

3. *Place bread slices on a cutting board then spread 1/2 tablespoon butter on one side of each bread slice.*

4. *Flip the bread slices over.*

5. *Spread mayonnaise on one bread slice.*

6. *Place remaining ingredients on top of the mayonnaise bread slice.*

7. *Top with other bread slice, butter-side up.*

8. *Place panini on the Tri-Grill; close lid.*

9. *Grill for 4-5 minutes or until bread is golden brown.*

10. *Remove, cut and serve.*

CHEESY PANINI

Makes 2 servings

Ingredients:
4 crusty bread slices
2 tablespoons softened unsalted butter
2 Provolone cheese slices
2 sharp Cheddar cheese slices
2 Monterey Jack cheese slices

Method:
1. *Fit the Tri-Grill with the upper and lower RIBBED GRILLING PLATES then set to CONTACT position.*
2. *To preheat, set the upper and lower temperature to 400°F.*
3. *Place the bread slices on a cutting board.*
4. *Spread 1/2 tablespoon butter on one side of each bread slice.*
5. *Flip the bread slices over.*
6. *Place 1 slice of each cheese on 2 bread slices.*
7. *Top each with another bread slice, butter-side up.*
8. *Place the panini on the Tri-Grill; close lid.*
9. *Cook for 3-5 minutes or until cheese is melted.*
10. *Remove and serve immediately.*

OPEN FACED MUSHROOM SANDWICH

Makes 1 serving

Ingredients:

1 Italian bread slice or other type of oval loaf, cut 2-inches thick

2 teaspoons unsalted butter, softened

6 cremini mushrooms, cleaned, trimmed and thinly sliced

1 teaspoon extra-virgin olive oil

Kosher salt and fresh pepper to taste

Method:

1. *Fit the Tri-Grill with the upper and lower RIBBED GRILLING PLATES then set to CONTACT position.*
2. *To preheat, set the upper and lower temperature to 450°F.*
3. *Spread butter on both sides of the bread slice.*
4. *Top bread slice with layers of mushroom slices.*
5. *Drizzle oil over mushrooms; season with salt and pepper.*
6. *Apply nonstick spray to the Tri-Grill.*
7. *Place sandwich on the Tri-Grill; close lid.*
8. *Grill for 4-5 minutes or until bread is toasted and mushrooms are browned.*
9. *Serve immediately.*

MINI BURGERS

Makes 10 burgers

Ingredients:
10 ounces lean ground beef
Kosher salt and fresh pepper to taste
Small buns

Method:
1. *Fit the Tri-Grill with the upper and lower RIBBED GRILLING PLATES then set to CONTACT position.*
2. *To preheat, set the upper and lower temperature to 450°F.*
3. *Shape meat into 10 equally sized patties then season to taste with salt and pepper.*
4. *Apply nonstick spray to the Tri-Grill.*
5. *Place 5 patties on the Tri-Grill; close lid.*
6. *Cook for 2-3 minutes or until desired doneness.*
7. *Repeat with remaining patties.*
8. *Serve on small buns with your favorite condiments.*

TIP
Any leftover mini burgers easily become wonderful meatballs in your favorite pasta sauce.

SNAPPER WITH WILTED SPINACH

Makes 4 servings

Ingredients:

4 (6 ounces each) snapper fillets or other white fish
Kosher salt and pepper to taste
2 tablespoons olive oil, divided
1 pound fresh spinach
2 tablespoons chicken stock or water
1 garlic clove, minced
2 teaspoons sesame seeds

Method:

1. Fit the Tri-Grill with the lower GRIDDLE PLATE and upper RIBBED GRILLING PLATE then set to DUAL position.
2. To preheat, set the lower temperature to 450°F.
3. Pat fish thoroughly dry using paper towels.
4. Season fish with salt and pepper.
5. Brush some oil onto the Tri-Grill.
6. Place fish on the Tri-Grill and cook for 3-4 minutes (depending on thickness of fish).
7. Flip over and cook the other side until brown and opaque inside (do not overcook).
8. Remove fish and keep warm.
9. Drizzle remaining oil onto the Tri-Grill then pile on all of the spinach; season with salt and pepper.
10. Drizzle spinach with the stock then sprinkle with garlic and sesame seeds.
11. Turn the spinach often using tongs (use caution to avoid the steam).
12. Cook spinach for 3-4 minutes or until wilted; remove immediately.
13. Divide the spinach between plates, top with fish and serve.

LAMB T-BONES WITH GARLIC BUTTER

Makes 4 servings

For The Garlic Butter:

4 tablespoons unsalted butter
4 garlic cloves
Kosher salt and pepper to taste
1 teaspoon fresh lemon zest
1 tablespoon fresh rosemary leaves

For The Lamb:

8 lamb loin chops

Method:

1. Fit the Tri-Grill with the lower GRIDDLE PLATE and upper RIBBED GRILLING PLATE then set to DUAL position.
2. To preheat, set the lower temperature to 450°F.
3. In a food processor, combine the butter, garlic, salt, pepper, zest and rosemary.
4. Pulse until the rosemary is chopped into small pieces.
5. Thoroughly pat the lamb dry using paper towels.
6. Reserve half of the garlic butter mixture for serving.
7. Brush the remaining mixture over all sides of the lamb.
8. Cook the lamb on the Tri-Grill for 3-5 minutes on each side or until desired doneness.
9. Remove to a platter and brush reserved garlic butter over the lamb.
10. Serve immediately.

TIP

Make some extra garlic butter and keep it in the freezer. A thin slice of this butter will really add flavor to chicken breasts. You can also make great, instant garlic bread.

FISH TOSTADAS

Makes 4 servings

For The Tostadas:
1 pound mild white fish fillets, such as tilapia
2 tablespoons canola oil
1 garlic clove, minced
1 teaspoon ground cumin
1 teaspoon chili powder
Kosher salt and pepper to taste

For Serving:
Corn tortillas, warmed
Salsa
Lettuce
Red onions
Condiments

Method:

1. *Fit the Tri-Grill with the upper and lower RIBBED GRILLING PLATES then set to DUAL position.*
2. *To preheat, set the upper and lower temperature to 350°F.*
3. *Pat fish completely dry using paper towels.*
4. *In a small bowl, stir together the oil, garlic, cumin and chili powder.*
5. *Season with salt and pepper then brush mixture on both sides of the fish.*
6. *Place fish on the Tri-Grill and cook until fish flakes apart but is still very moist (turn once during cooking).*
7. *Transfer fish to a plate and flake apart.*
8. *Serve in warm tortillas with desired toppings.*

TIP
Any mild white fish will work well in this recipe.

CHEESE STUFFED BURGERS

Makes 4 servings

Ingredients:

1 3/4 pounds ground beef
2 ounces Cheddar cheese, shredded and divided
Kosher salt and pepper to taste
4 soft burger buns
4 lettuce leaves
4 tomato slices
4 red onion slices

Method:

1. *Divide beef into 8 equal portions.*
2. *On a baking sheet, shape each portion into a 4 1/2-inch diameter patty.*
3. *Using your thumb, make a small indentation into each patty.*
4. *Place 1/2-ounce of cheese into the indentation of the four patties.*
5. *Season each patty with salt and pepper.*
6. *Top each with another patty and press all around the edges to seal.*
7. *Fit the Tri-Grill with the upper and lower RIBBED GRILLING PLATES then set to CONTACT position.*
8. *To preheat, set the upper and lower temperature to 400°F.*
9. *Place burgers on the Tri-Grill; close lid.*
10. *Cook for 5-6 minutes or until desired doneness.*
11. *Place patties on buns, top with lettuce, tomatoes, onions as well as your favorite condiments before serving.*

BIG BREAKFAST FRY UP

Makes 2 servings

Ingredients:

4 raw bacon slices, cut into 1-inch strips
1 medium Russet potato, peeled and diced small
1/2 small yellow onion, diced
1/2 cup button mushrooms, sliced
Kosher salt and pepper to taste
4 large eggs
Buttered toast, for serving

Method:

1. *Fit the Tri-Grill with the lower GRIDDLE PLATE and upper RIBBED GRILLING PLATE then set to DUAL position.*
2. *To preheat, set the lower temperature to 350°F.*
3. *Place bacon on the Tri-Grill and toss.*
4. *When some bacon grease appears on the Tri-Grill, add the potatoes, onions and mushrooms.*
5. *Season with salt and pepper and turn frequently.*
6. *When potatoes, onions and mushrooms are browned and potatoes are tender, remove to a platter, leaving the bacon grease on the Tri-Grill.*
7. *Crack the eggs onto the Tri-Grill, one at a time.*
8. *Season with salt and pepper and cook until desired doneness.*
9. *Garnish as desired and serve with toast.*

TIP

This dish is a great place to use up
leftovers such as cheese, bell peppers, peas,
ham or lunch meats.

SPAGHETTI PANCAKES

Makes 4 servings

Ingredients:

1 bunch green onions, thinly sliced
2 tablespoons all purpose flour
2 tablespoons Parmesan cheese, grated
4 large eggs
Kosher salt and pepper to taste
1/4 cup bell peppers, diced
8 ounces spaghetti noodles, cooked and cooled
3 tablespoons unsalted butter, melted and divided

Method:

1. *Fit the Tri-Grill with the lower GRIDDLE PLATE and upper RIBBED GRILLING PLATE then set to DUAL position.*
2. *To preheat, set the lower temperature to 350°F.*
3. *In a large bowl, combine the green onions, flour, cheese, eggs, salt, pepper and bell peppers; mix thoroughly then add the pasta to the bowl.*
4. *Drizzle some melted butter onto the Tri-Grill.*
5. *Spoon mounds of mixture onto the Tri-Grill, pat each down slightly and cook for 4 minutes on each side or until well browned.*
6. *Remove and repeat with remaining mixture.*
7. *Garnish as desired and serve hot.*

TIP

This recipe works well with any leftover pasta and is a great way to use up any leftover vegetables.

BASIC CREPES

Makes 12 servings

Ingredients:

3/4 cup water
3/4 cup whole milk
1 cup all purpose flour
3 large eggs
2 tablespoons unsalted butter, melted
1 tablespoon granulated sugar
1/2 teaspoon kosher salt
Canola oil

Method:

1. Fit the Tri-Grill with the lower GRIDDLE PLATE and upper RIBBED GRILLING PLATE then set to DUAL position.
2. To preheat, set the lower temperature to 450°F.
3. In a blender combine all ingredients, except canola oil.
4. Blend until smooth then set aside.
5. Using a paper towel, wipe a small amount of oil onto the GRIDDLE PLATE.
6. Using a ladle, pour 2 tablespoons of batter onto the GRIDDLE PLATE.
7. Quickly use the bottom of the ladle to spread the batter thinly using a circular motion.
8. Cook for about 1-2 minutes then use a small off-set spatula to flip the crepes over.
9. Cook for an additional 10 seconds then transfer to a plate.
10. Repeat with any remaining batter.
11. Fill and serve as desired.

INDIVIDUAL PIZZAS

Makes 4 servings

Ingredients:

1 pound store-bought pizza dough
1/4 cup jarred pesto
1/4 cup red onions, thinly sliced
1/2 cup pepperoni or sausage
1/4 cup sun dried tomatoes, julienned
1/4 cup button mushrooms, shaved
1/4 cup grape tomatoes, sliced
1 cup mozzarella cheese, shredded
1 cup fresh milk mozzarella, diced
Kosher salt and fresh pepper to taste
2 teaspoons fresh thyme sprigs

Method:

1. *Fit the Tri-Grill with the lower GRIDDLE PLATE and upper RIBBED GRILLING PLATE then set to CONTACT position.*
2. *To preheat, set the upper temperature to 400°F and lower temperature to 300°F.*
3. *Cut the dough into 8 pieces and stretch each piece into a small circle.*
4. *Place as many dough circles onto the Tri-Grill as will fit; close lid.*
5. *Cook for 2-4 minutes or until lightly browned.*
6. *Remove and repeat with any remaining dough circles.*
7. *Set Tri-Grill to FIXED position.*
8. *Top each pizza crust with remaining ingredients as desired.*
9. *Place as many pizzas on the Tri-Grill as will fit; lower lid.*
10. *Cook for 4-5 minutes or until cheese is bubbly.*
11. *Remove, repeat with remaining pizzas and serve hot.*

CHEESY SPINACH CREPES

Makes 4 servings

Ingredients:

1 prepared recipe Basic Crepes (see page 84)
1 tablespoon unsalted butter
1 small yellow onion, diced
1 bag (9 oz.) fresh baby spinach
Kosher salt and fresh pepper to taste
A few dashes of bottled hot pepper sauce
1 teaspoon dry mustard powder
2 teaspoons soy sauce
1 cup heavy cream
1 1/2 cups Swiss cheese, grated + more for topping
1/4 cup Parmesan cheese, grated + more for topping

Method:

1. *In a sauté pan on the stovetop over medium-high heat, combine the butter and onions; sauté until brown.*
2. *Add the spinach, salt, pepper, hot sauce, mustard powder and soy sauce; stir until wilted.*
3. *Add the heavy cream, Swiss cheese and Parmesan cheese; stir until well blended and cheese is melted.*
4. *Fit the Tri-Grill with the lower GRIDDLE PLATE and upper RIBBED GRILLING PLATE then set to FIXED position.*
5. *To preheat, set the upper and lower temperature to 450°F.*
6. *Divide the mixture between 12 prepared crepes, roll them up then place them all into a greased baking dish.*
7. *Top with additional Swiss and Parmesan cheese.*
8. *Place baking dish on the Tri-Grill; lower lid.*
9. *Cook for 12-15 minutes or until the filling is very hot and the cheese has browned.*
10. *Serve immediately.*

CHOCOLATE BLINTZES

Makes 4 servings

For The Batter:

3/4 cup water
3/4 cup whole milk
1 cup all purpose flour
2 tablespoons cocoa powder
3 large eggs
2 tablespoons unsalted butter, melted
1 tablespoon granulated sugar
1/2 teaspoon kosher salt
Canola oil

For The Filling:

1 cup Farmer's or ricotta cheese
1 package (8 oz.) cream cheese, softened
1 teaspoon vanilla extract
1/3 cup dark cocoa powder
1 cup powdered sugar
1 cup white chocolate chips
4 tablespoons unsalted butter, melted

Method:

1. *Fit the Tri-Grill with the lower GRIDDLE PLATE and upper RIBBED GRILLING PLATE then set to DUAL position.*

2. *To preheat, set the lower temperature to 450°F.*

3. *In a blender combine all batter ingredients, except canola oil; blend until smooth then set aside.*

4. *Using a paper towel, wipe a small amount of oil onto the GRIDDLE PLATE then use a ladle to pour 2 tablespoons of batter onto the GRIDDLE PLATE.*

5. *Quickly use the bottom of the ladle to spread the batter thinly using a circular motion.*

6. *Cook for 1-2 minutes then use a small off-set spatula to flip over; cook for an additional 10 seconds.*

7. *Transfer to a plate then repeat with any remaining batter.*

8. *In a bowl combine the cheeses, vanilla, dark cocoa powder and sugar then mix well.*

9. *Fold in the white chocolate chips then transfer the mixture to a pastry bag fitted with a large plain tip; pipe mixture evenly onto the center of 8 blintzes.*

10. *Roll each of the blintzes up like a burrito and place seam-side down onto the Tri-Grill; drizzle all tops with the melted butter.*

11. *When undersides are brown and crispy, flip and cook until the other side is brown.*

12. *Remove and serve with desired toppings.*

CHICKEN & BACON BURGERS

Makes 4 servings

Ingredients:

12 ounces ground chicken
Kosher salt and pepper to taste
12 bacon slices, uncooked
4 soft buns
Lettuce and tomatoes, for serving

Method:

1. *Divide the ground chicken into 4 equal patties.*
2. *Season patties with salt and pepper.*
3. *Lay three strips of bacon in a criss-cross fashion over the top of each patty.*
4. *Neatly tuck the bacon ends under each patty.*
5. *Fit the Tri-Grill with the upper and lower RIBBED GRILLING PLATES then set to CONTACT position.*
6. *To preheat, set the upper and lower temperature to 400°F.*
7. *Place the patties on the Tri-Grill; close lid.*
8. *Cook for 5-6 minutes or until internal temperature reaches 165°F on a meat thermometer.*
9. *Serve on buns with lettuce and tomatoes.*

BBQ CHICKEN

Makes 4 servings

For The Chicken:
4 pounds meaty chicken pieces such as breasts, thighs and legs
Kosher salt and pepper to taste

For The BBQ Sauce:
1/4 cup honey
1 cup favorite bottled BBQ sauce
1/4 cup yellow mustard
1 small yellow onion, minced

Method:

1. *Fit the Tri-Grill with the upper and lower RIBBED GRILLING PLATES then set to DUAL position.*

2. *To preheat, set the upper and lower temperature to 300°F.*

3. *Thoroughly pat dry the chicken using paper towels.*

4. *Season the chicken with salt and pepper.*

5. *Place chicken on the Tri-Grill and cook for 8-10 minutes.*

6. *While cooking the chicken, combine all BBQ sauce ingredients in a sauce pan on the Tri-Grill or on the stovetop over medium heat; bring to a gentle simmer and cook for 5 minutes then set aside.*

7. *Flip chicken over and cook the other side for 8-10 minutes.*

8. *When chicken reaches 130°F on a meat thermometer, brush with BBQ sauce.*

9. *Increase upper and lower Tri-Grill temperature to 450°F and cook for a few additional minutes until sauce caramelizes and temperature reaches 165°F on a meat thermometer.*

10. *Serve immediately.*

MEXICAN STYLE CHICKEN

Makes 4 servings

Ingredients:

4 medium chicken breasts, patted dry
Zest and juice from 1 lime
2 teaspoons dried chipotle chili powder
2 garlic cloves, minced
Kosher salt to taste
1 tablespoon canola oil

Method:

1. *Fit the Tri-Grill with the upper and lower RIBBED GRILLING PLATES then set to CONTACT position.*
2. *To preheat, set the upper and lower temperature to 450°F.*
3. *Sprinkle each chicken breast with lime zest, juice, chipotle, garlic and salt.*
4. *Drizzle both sides of the chicken breasts with oil.*
5. *Place chicken on the Tri-Grill; close lid.*
6. *Cook for 5-6 minutes or until internal temperature reaches 165°F on a meat thermometer.*
7. *Garnish as desired and serve.*

TIP

I suggest investing in a good, instant-read thermometer. I like the kind that has a small reference on the back showing what temperatures are correct for meat, poultry, pork, shellfish and fish. You can find these at any kitchen type store.

SKEWERED SALMON

Makes 4 servings

For The Salmon:

4 salmon fillets (4 ounces each), cut into 1-inch wide strips
2 lemons, cut into thin slices
8 bamboo skewers (8-inch long)
Canola oil, for brushing
Kosher salt and pepper to taste
2 tablespoons fresh dill, chopped

For The Cucumber Salad:

2 English cucumbers, diced
1/2 small red onion, diced
3 tablespoons feta cheese, crumbled
2 tablespoons olive oil
2 tablespoons white wine vinegar
Kosher salt and pepper to taste

Method:

1. *Fit the Tri-Grill with the upper and lower RIBBED GRILLING PLATES then set to DUAL position.*
2. *To preheat, set the upper and lower temperature to 350°F.*
3. *Weave 2 salmon strips onto each skewer, alternating with lemon slices.*
4. *Brush skewers with oil then season with salt and pepper.*
5. *Place skewers on the Tri-Grill and cook 3-4 minutes per side (do not overcook the salmon).*
6. *In a large bowl, combine all salad ingredients; toss well.*
7. *Garnish salmon skewers with dill and serve with the cucumber salad.*

CHEESE BLINTZES

Makes 4 servings

Ingredients:

1 prepared recipe Basic Crepes (see page 84)
1 cup Farmer's or ricotta cheese
1 package (8 oz.) cream cheese, softened
1/2 teaspoon fresh lemon zest
2 teaspoons fresh lemon juice
1/4 teaspoon vanilla extract
1 cup powdered sugar
1 cup red cherry preserves
4 tablespoons unsalted butter, melted
Sour cream, for serving
Powdered sugar, for serving

Method:

1. *Fit the Tri-Grill with the lower GRIDDLE PLATE and upper RIBBED GRILLING PLATE then set to DUAL position.*

2. *To preheat, set the lower temperature to 450°F.*

3. *In a bowl, combine the cheeses, lemon zest and juice, vanilla and sugar.*

4. *Mix until smooth then transfer to a pastry bag.*

5. *Pipe mixture evenly onto the center of 8 crepes.*

6. *Top mixture with a spoonful of cherry preserves.*

7. *Roll up the blintzes by folding in the sides then rolling up like a burrito.*

8. *Place the blintzes, seam-side down, onto the Tri-Grill.*

9. *Drizzle the tops of the blintzes with butter.*

10. *Cook until the bottoms are brown and crisp then turn to brown the other side of the blintzes.*

11. *Remove blintzes to serving plates then top with sour cream, additional cherry preserves and a sprinkle of powdered sugar.*

12. *Serve immediately.*

CREAMY SPINACH PIZZA

Makes 2 pizzas

Ingredients:

1 pound prepared pizza dough, divided
1/2 cup heavy cream
2 tablespoons sour cream
1/3 cup Parmesan cheese, grated
2 garlic cloves
1 cup fresh baby spinach leaves
Kosher salt and fresh pepper to taste
1/2 cup mozzarella cheese, shredded
1/2 teaspoon dried thyme leaves

RECIPES

Method:

1. *Fit the Tri-Grill with the lower GRIDDLE PLATE and upper RIBBED GRILLING PLATE then set to FIXED position.*
2. *To preheat, set the upper and lower temperature to 450°F.*
3. *On a floured surface, stretch out each pizza dough ball into a rough 8-inch square.*
4. *Place each pizza dough on a piece of parchment paper cut to fit the Tri-Grill.*
5. *In a bowl, combine the heavy cream, sour cream, cheese, garlic and spinach; purée using an immersion blender.*
6. *Season the sauce with salt and pepper.*
7. *Spread 3 tablespoons of sauce on top of each dough square (you will have extra sauce left over).*
8. *Top sauce with mozzarella cheese and thyme.*
9. *Lift a pizza with the parchment and place on the Tri-Grill.*
10. *Lower the lid and cook pizza for 5-6 minutes or until cheese is well browned and bottom crust is very brown.*
11. *Repeat with other pizza and serve.*

SWEET POTATO WITH MARSHMALLOW

Makes 4 servings

Ingredients:

2 tablespoons sugar
1 teaspoon ground cinnamon
1 medium sweet potato, peeled and cut into 1/2-inch slices
Olive oil
6 large marshmallows

Method:

1. *Fit the Tri-Grill with the lower GRIDDLE PLATE and upper RIBBED GRILLING PLATE then set to CONTACT position.*
2. *To preheat, set the upper and lower temperature to 400°F.*
3. *In a small bowl, combine the sugar and cinnamon.*
4. *Brush 6 sweet potato slices with olive oil.*
5. *Place potato slices on the Tri-Grill; close lid.*
6. *Cook for 3-5 minutes or until tender.*
7. *Lift the lid and sprinkle the sugar mixture onto the sweet potato slices.*
8. *Place a marshmallow on top of each slice.*
9. *Set Tri-Grill to FIXED position, lower the lid and cook for 3-4 minutes or until marshmallows starts to melt.*
10. *Remove and serve immediately.*

EASY CHOCOLATE CREPES

Makes 4 servings

For The Crepes:
1 1/2 cups whole milk
3/4 cup all purpose flour
6 tablespoons cocoa powder
3 large eggs
1/4 cup granulated sugar
3 tablespoons unsalted butter, melted
1 teaspoon vanilla extract
1/2 teaspoon kosher salt
Canola oil

For Serving:
2 cups fresh raspberries
Sweetened whipped cream
Chocolate curls
Powdered sugar

Method:
1. *In a blender combine the milk, flour, cocoa, eggs, sugar, butter, vanilla and salt.*
2. *Blend until smooth then set aside.*
3. *Fit the Tri-Grill with the lower GRIDDLE PLATE and upper RIBBED GRILLING PLATE then set to DUAL position.*
4. *To preheat, set the lower temperature to 450°F.*
5. *Using a paper towel, wipe a small amount of oil onto the GRIDDLE PLATE.*
6. *Ladle 2 tablespoons batter onto the GRIDDLE PLATE.*
7. *Quickly use the bottom of the ladle to spread the batter in a circular motion.*
8. *Cook for about 1 minute then use a small off-set spatula to flip the crepes over.*
9. *Cook for an additional 10 seconds then transfer to a plate.*
10. *Repeat with remaining batter.*
11. *Fill crepes with raspberries and whipped cream, fold over then top with chocolate curls and powdered sugar.*

GRILLED VEGGIES WITH THYME

Makes 4 servings

Ingredients:

1 small eggplant, sliced 1/2-inch thick
1 red onion, sliced 1/2-inch thick
1 zucchini, sliced 1/2-inch thick
1 yellow squash, sliced 1/2-inch thick
1 large tomato, sliced 1/2-inch thick
2 tablespoons olive oil
2 garlic cloves, minced
1 teaspoon fresh thyme leaves
Kosher salt and pepper to taste

Method:

1. *Fit the Tri-Grill with the upper and lower RIBBED GRILLING PLATES then set to DUAL position.*
2. *To preheat, set the upper and lower temperature to 450°F.*
3. *Place vegetables in a mixing bowl.*
4. *Add oil, garlic and thyme to the bowl.*
5. *Season to taste with salt and pepper then toss to coat.*
6. *Place vegetables on the Tri-Grill and cook for 3-5 minutes on each side or until browned.*
7. *Remove and repeat with any remaining vegetables.*
8. *Serve hot.*

TIP
You can use any vegetables you have on hand. This is a great way to use up vegetables from the garden.

STRAWBERRY CHEESECAKE FRENCH TOAST

Makes 4 servings

Ingredients:

1 package (8 ounces) cream cheese, softened
1/4 cup strawberry jam
1 cup fresh strawberries, sliced
4 large eggs
1 1/2 cups half & half
8 thick French bread slices
3 tablespoons unsalted butter, melted and divided

Method:

1. *Fit the Tri-Grill with the lower GRIDDLE PLATE and upper RIBBED GRILLING PLATE then set to DUAL position.*
2. *To preheat, set the lower temperature to 350°F.*
3. *In a small bowl, combine the cream cheese and jam; stir until smooth.*
4. *Fold the strawberries into the cream cheese mixture then set aside.*
5. *In a shallow bowl, whisk together the eggs and half & half.*
6. *Dip the bread slices in egg mixture and place on the Tri-Grill.*
7. *Drizzle with half of the melted butter and cook for 3 minutes or until golden brown.*
8. *Flip over, drizzle with remaining butter and cook for an additional 3 minutes.*
9. *Remove to serving plates and top with strawberry mixture.*
10. *Garnish as desired and serve hot.*

TIP

This recipe works well with any berries and even diced peaches.

ABC - 123
PANCAKES

Makes 4 servings

Ingredients:

2 cups all purpose flour
2 teaspoons baking powder
2 tablespoons granulated sugar
1 teaspoon kosher salt
2 cups whole milk
2 large eggs
2 tablespoons canola oil
Food coloring
Plastic squeeze bottles

Method:

1. *Fit the Tri-Grill with the lower GRIDDLE PLATE and upper RIBBED GRILLING PLATE then set to DUAL position.*

2. *To preheat, set the lower temperature to 350°F.*

3. *In a bowl, whisk together the flour, baking powder, sugar and salt.*

4. *In a separate bowl, whisk together the milk, eggs and oil.*

5. *Pour the milk mixture into the flour mixture and whisk until fairly smooth.*

6. *Pour 1 cup of batter back into the emptied milk bowl.*

7. *Stir in the food coloring of your choice until desired color is achieved.*

8. *Pour the colored batter into a plastic squeeze bottle.*

9. *Pour the white batter into a separate plastic squeeze bottle.*

10. *Using the colored batter, pipe letters or numbers directly onto the Tri-Grill.*

11. *Using the white batter, squeeze a pancake over the letters or numbers on the Tri-Grill.*

12. *When bubbles form on the pancake surface, flip over and cook for 1-2 minutes or until golden brown.*

13. *Remove and repeat with remaining batter, making multiple pancakes on the Tri-Grill at the same time.*

EGGS IN PEPPER RINGS

Makes 4 servings

Ingredients:

1 very large green bell pepper
1 tablespoon unsalted butter, divided
1 small tomato, diced
1 green onion, sliced
4 large eggs
Kosher salt and pepper to taste

Method:

1. *Fit the Tri-Grill with the lower GRIDDLE PLATE and upper RIBBED GRILLING PLATE then set to DUAL position.*
2. *To preheat, set the lower temperature to 350°F.*
3. *Slice the bell pepper into 4 even and straight rings, 1/2-inch thick each.*
4. *Place bell pepper rings on the Tri-Grill and drop a small amount of butter into each ring.*
5. *Scatter some diced tomato into each bell pepper ring, reserving some for garnish.*
6. *Scatter greens onions into each bell pepper ring.*
7. *Crack an egg into each bell pepper ring (don't worry if some egg white runs out).*
8. *Season eggs with salt and pepper.*
9. *When most of the egg whites have set, flip over and cook the second sides until desired doneness (for sunny side up eggs, cook until egg white is set and do not flip over).*
10. *Remove, garnish with remaining tomatoes and serve.*

TIP

Add some bacon or breakfast sausages to the grill side to make a complete breakfast.

PEPPERONI
PIZZA

Makes two 8-inch pizzas

For The Crust:
1 pound store-bought pizza dough ball, divided
1 tablespoon olive oil

Toppings:
1/4 cup prepared marinara sauce or pesto
1 cup mozzarella cheese, shredded
20 pepperoni slices
2 tablespoons Parmesan cheese, grated
Basil leaves

Method:

1. *Fit the Tri-Grill with the lower GRIDDLE PLATE and upper RIBBED GRILLING PLATE then set to CONTACT position.*
2. *To preheat, set the upper temperature to 400°F and lower temperature to 300°F.*
3. *Stretch each pizza dough ball into a rough 8-inch circle.*
4. *Lightly brush all sides with oil.*
5. *Place a pizza dough crust onto the Tri-Grill; close lid.*
6. *Cook for 3-4 minutes or until desired doneness.*
7. *Open the lid, top with half of the toppings in the order listed above.*
8. *Set Tri-Grill to the FIXED position and lower the lid.*
9. *Cook for 4 minutes then check the underside of the pizza and remove when it is well browned.*
10. *Repeat with remaining ingredients to make another pizza.*

SHRIMP CAKES

Makes 4 servings

Ingredients:

2 Italian bread slices, crusts removed
1 pound fresh shrimp, chopped
2 tablespoons mayonnaise
1/2 teaspoon fresh lemon zest
2 teaspoons fresh lemon juice
1 teaspoon kosher salt
3 green onions, sliced
1 tablespoon bell peppers, diced small

Method:

1. *Fit the Tri-Grill with the lower GRIDDLE PLATE and upper RIBBED GRILLING PLATE then set to DUAL position.*

2. *To preheat, set the lower temperature to 350°F.*

3. *Place the bread into a food processor and pulse until coarse crumbs are achieved (or tear into very small pieces using your hands).*

4. *Place the breadcrumbs and remaining ingredients into a large bowl.*

5. *Using a spatula, gently fold the ingredients together.*

6. *Divide the mixture into 4 portions and gently shape into patties.*

7. *Place patties on the Tri-Grill and cook for 4-5 minutes on each side or until golden brown.*

8. *Garnish as desired and serve immediately.*

BREAKFAST OMELET

Makes 2 servings

Ingredients:

4 large eggs
1 tablespoon half & half
Kosher salt and pepper to taste
1 1/2 teaspoons unsalted butter, softened
1 green onion, thinly sliced
1/4 cup cooked and crumbled breakfast sausage
1/2 cup Cheddar cheese, shredded

Method:

1. *Fit the Tri-Grill with the lower GRIDDLE PLATE and upper RIBBED GRILLING PLATE then set to DUAL position.*
2. *To preheat, set the lower temperature to 350°F.*
3. *In a bowl, combine the eggs, half & half, salt and pepper; whisk until color is uniform.*
4. *Brush the butter onto the GRIDDLE PLATE.*
5. *Pour the egg mixture onto the GRIDDLE PLATE.*
6. *Spread out evenly using a silicone spatula.*
7. *Cook until mostly set then scatter remaining ingredients over the omelet.*
8. *Using the spatula, begin to roll up the omelet starting on the short side.*
9. *When you finished rolling up the omelet, lift it off the Tri-Grill using two spatulas.*
10. *Cut omelet into 4 slices, garnish as desired and serve.*

TIP

For an interesting twist, add a bit of marinara sauce, pepperoni and a sprinkle of mozzarella cheese.

BLUEBERRIES & CREAM PANCAKES

Makes 4 servings

Ingredients:

2 cups fresh blueberries, divided
1 package (8 ounces) cream cheese, softened
1 cup powdered sugar
2 cups all purpose flour
2 teaspoons baking powder
1 teaspoon kosher salt
2 tablespoons granulated sugar
2 cups buttermilk or whole milk
2 large eggs
2 tablespoons canola oil

Method:

1. *Fit the Tri-Grill with the lower GRIDDLE PLATE and upper RIBBED GRILLING PLATE then set to DUAL position.*
2. *To preheat, set the lower temperature to 350°F.*
3. *In a bowl, combine 1 cup of blueberries, cream cheese and powdered sugar; set aside.*
4. *In a separate bowl, whisk together the flour, baking powder, salt and sugar.*
5. *In a third bowl, whisk together the milk, eggs and oil.*
6. *Pour milk mixture over the flour mixture and whisk until fairly smooth.*
7. *Ladle as many pancakes as will fit onto the Tri-Grill.*
8. *When bubbles form on the surface, flip pancakes over and cook until golden brown.*
9. *Repeat with remaining batter.*
10. *To serve, layer pancakes with cream cheese mixture and additional blueberries.*
11. *Garnish as desired and serve.*

TIP

You can use inexpensive plastic squeeze bottles to squeeze the pancakes onto the griddle.

SCALLOPS WITH PINEAPPLE SALAD

Makes 4 servings

Ingredients:

4 tablespoons fresh lime juice
6 tablespoons Asian chili sauce, divided
Kosher salt and pepper to taste
16 sea scallops, thawed and patted dry
1/3 cup canola oil
2 tablespoons fresh cilantro, chopped
3 tablespoons white wine vinegar
4 cups fresh baby spinach
1 cup fresh pineapple chunks
1/4 cup red onions, chopped

Method:

1. *Fit the Tri-Grill with the lower GRIDDLE PLATE and upper RIBBED GRILLING PLATE then set to DUAL position.*
2. *To preheat, set the lower temperature to 450°F.*
3. *In a bowl, combine the lime juice, 4 tablespoons chili sauce, salt and pepper; stir.*
4. *Brush scallops with sauce then place them onto the Tri-Grill.*
5. *Cook scallops for 3-4 minutes on each side until opaque or until desired doneness.*
6. *In a bowl, combine remaining chili sauce, oil, cilantro and vinegar.*
7. *Add the spinach, pineapple and onions to the bowl; toss to coat.*
8. *Season with salt and pepper then divide the salad between 4 plates.*
9. *Place 4 scallops on each salad and serve.*

TIP

When you buy scallops, remove the small, flat piece of adductor muscle that often lies beside the scallop. Just pull it off with your fingers. It is unpleasantly chewy if you leave it on.

SWORDFISH WITH MANGO SALSA

Makes 4 servings

Ingredients:

1 firm mango, peeled and diced

1/2 small red onion, chopped small

Juice of 1 lime

Minced jalapeño peppers to taste

Kosher salt and pepper to taste

2 tablespoons fresh cilantro, chopped

2 tablespoons olive oil, divided

4 (6 ounces each) swordfish steaks

Method:

1. *Fit the Tri-Grill with the lower GRIDDLE PLATE and upper RIBBED GRILLING PLATE then set to DUAL position.*
2. *To preheat, set the lower temperature to 450°F.*
3. *In a bowl, combine the mango, red onions and lime juice; stir well.*
4. *Add the jalapeño, salt, pepper, cilantro and 1 tablespoon oil; set aside.*
5. *Thoroughly pat dry the fish using paper towels then season with salt and pepper.*
6. *Drizzle remaining oil onto the Tri-Grill.*
7. *Place fish on the Tri-Grill and cook for 3-4 minutes (depending on thickness of fish).*
8. *Flip over and cook the other side until brown and opaque inside (do not overcook).*
9. *Serve immediately with mango salsa.*

TIP

Before buying fish, check online for the sustainability of that particular fish. My favorite source for this information is the Monterrey Bay Aquarium. They also have a wonderful app if you have a smart phone.

SOURCE PAGE

Here are some of my favorite places to find ingredients that are not readily available at grocery stores as well as kitchen tools and supplies that help you become a better cook.

The Bakers Catalogue at King Arthur Flour

135 Route 5 South
P.O. Box 1010
Norwich, VT 05055

Pure fruit oils, citric acid, silicone spatulas, digital timers, oven thermometers, real truffle oil, off-set spatulas, measuring cups and spoons, knives, ice cream scoops, cheesecloth, cookie sheets, baking pans
www.kingarthurflour.com

Chocosphere

P.O. Box 2237
Tualatin, OR 97062
877-992-4623

Excellent quality cocoa (Callebaut)
All Chocolates
Jimmies and sprinkles
www.chocosphere.com

Gluten Free Mall

4927 Sonoma HWY Suite C1
Santa Rosa, CA 95409
707-509-4528

All ingredients needed for gluten-free baking
www.glutenfreemall.com

Body By Bison

www.hsn.com
Keyword: Body By Bison
Individually wrapped bison burger patties
www.hsn.com

D & G Occasions

625 Herndon Ave.
Orlando, FL 32803
407-894-4458

My favorite butter vanilla extract by
Magic Line, cake and candy making
supplies, citric acid, pure fruit oils,
professional food colorings, ultra thin
flexible spatulas, large selection of
sprinkles and jimmies, unusual birthday
candles, pure vanilla extract, pastry bags
and tips, parchment, off-set spatulas,
oven and candy thermometers, kitchen
timers, meat mallets, large selection of
cookie cutters
www.dandgoccasions.com

Penzeys Spices

P.O. Box 924
Brookfield, WI 53045
800-741-7787

Spices, extracts, seasonings, seasonal
cookie cutters, mallets and more
www.penzeys.com

INDEX

FOR ALL OF MARIAN GETZ'S COOKBOOKS AS WELL AS
COOKWARE, APPLIANCES, CUTLERY AND KITCHEN ACCESSORIES
BY WOLFGANG PUCK

PLEASE VISIT HSN.COM
(KEYWORD: WOLFGANG PUCK)